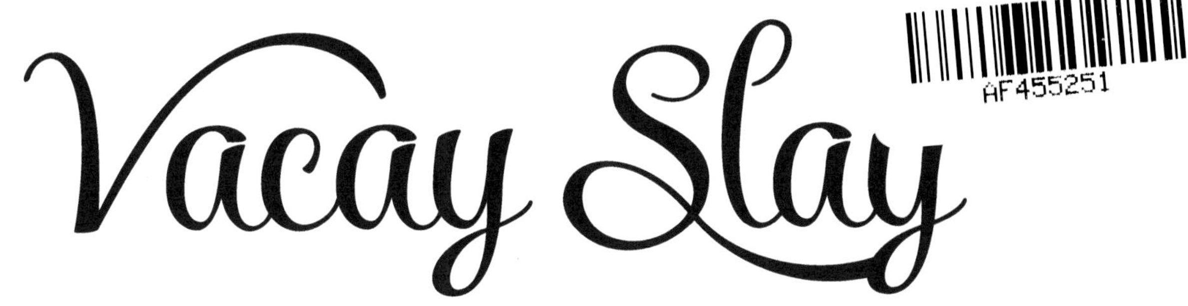

An Adult Coloring Book for Women Who Love to Travel!

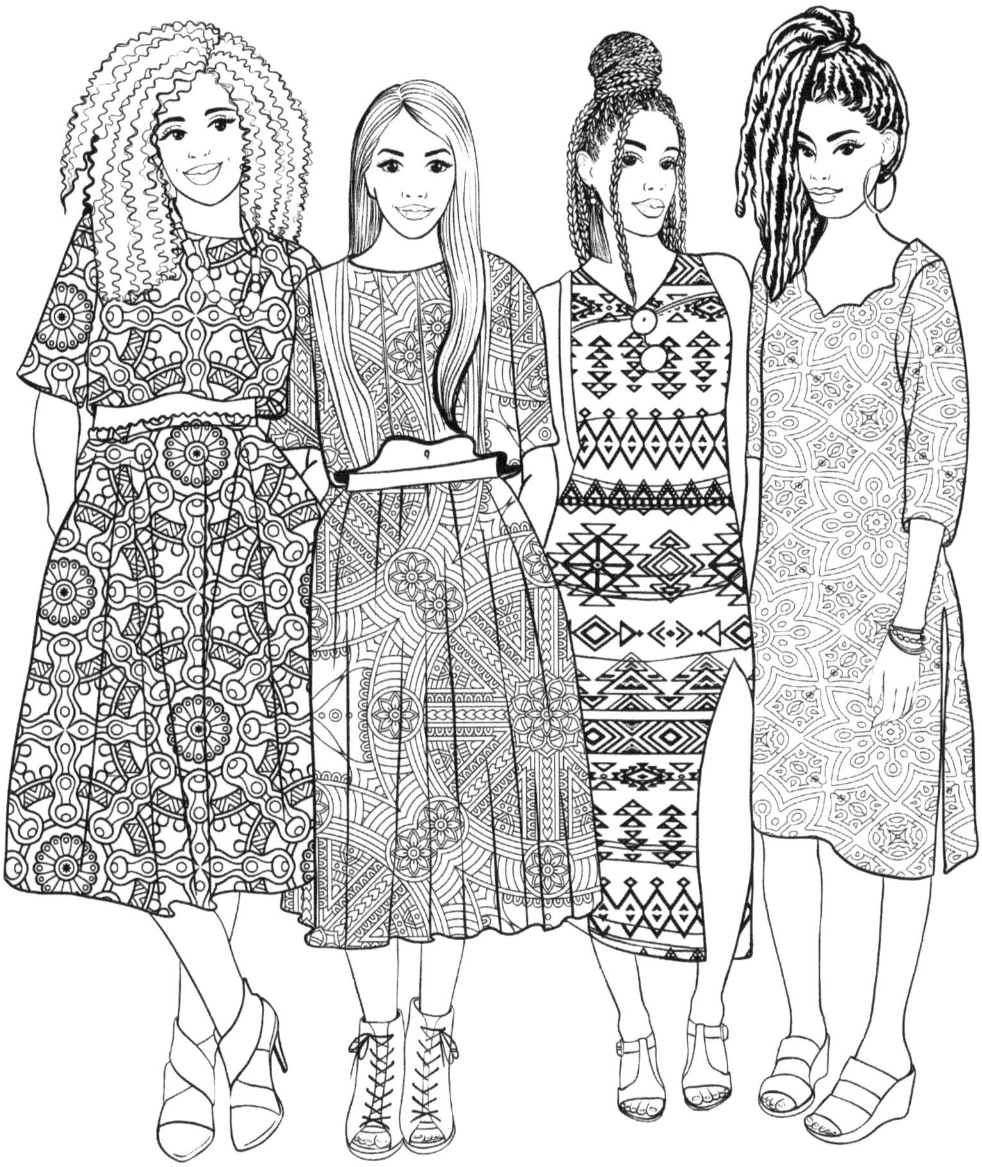

SHAYLA MCGHEE

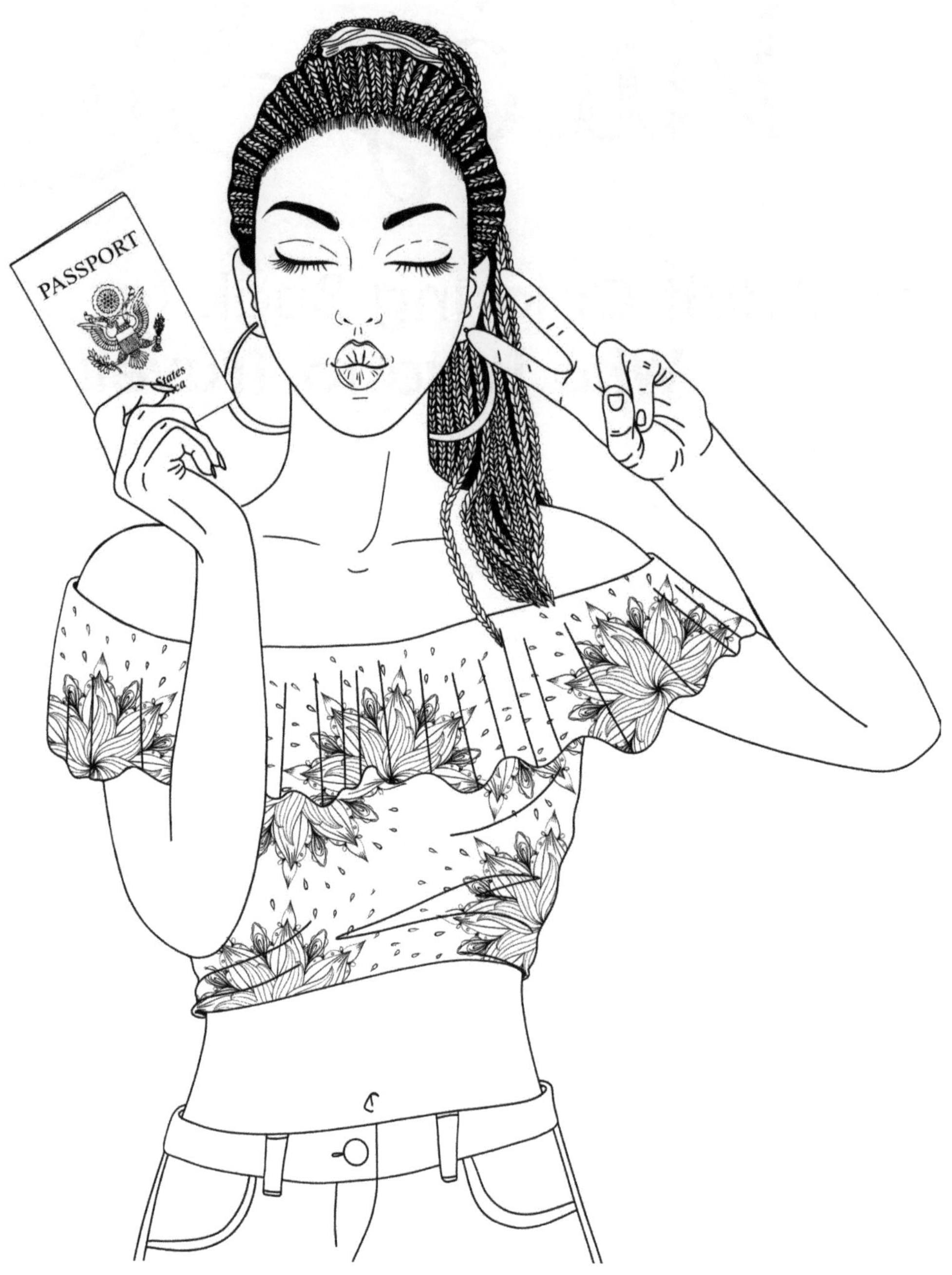

ISBN: 978-1-7345460-6-4

For more of our books, visit us online at sableinspiredbooks.com
Instagram: @sableinspiredbooks
Facebook: facebook.com/sableinspiredbooks

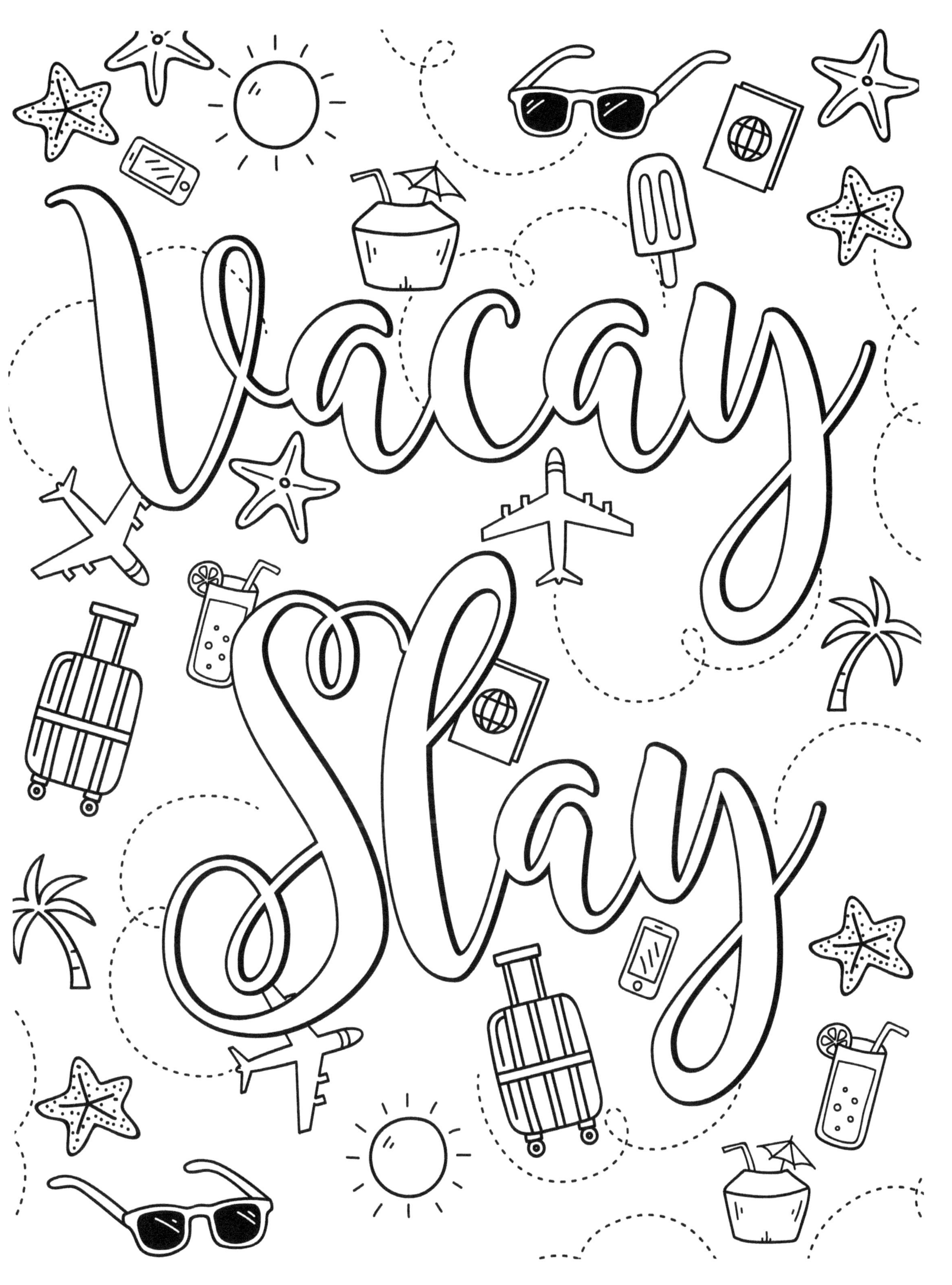
Vacay
Slay

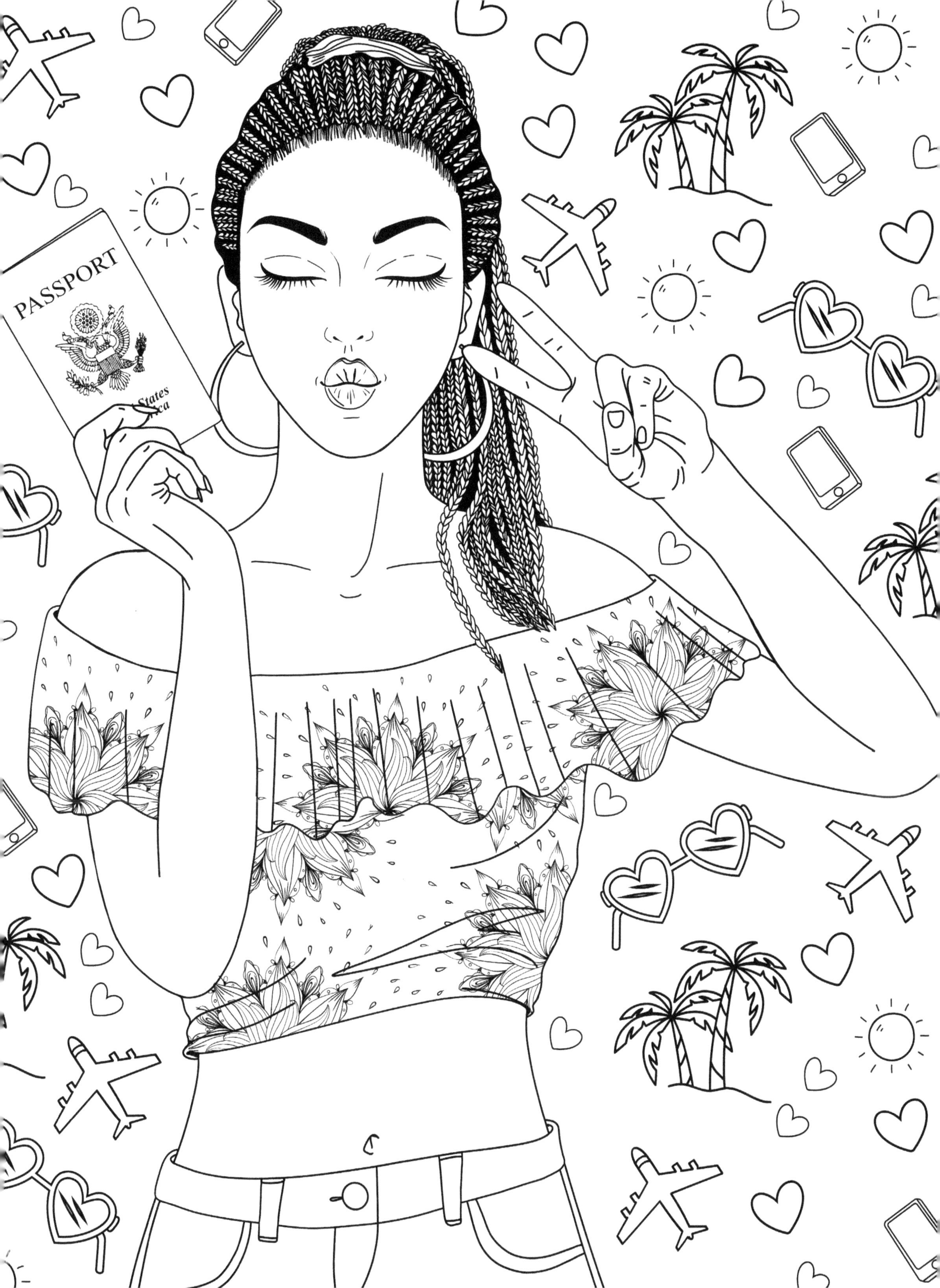
PASSPORT
States

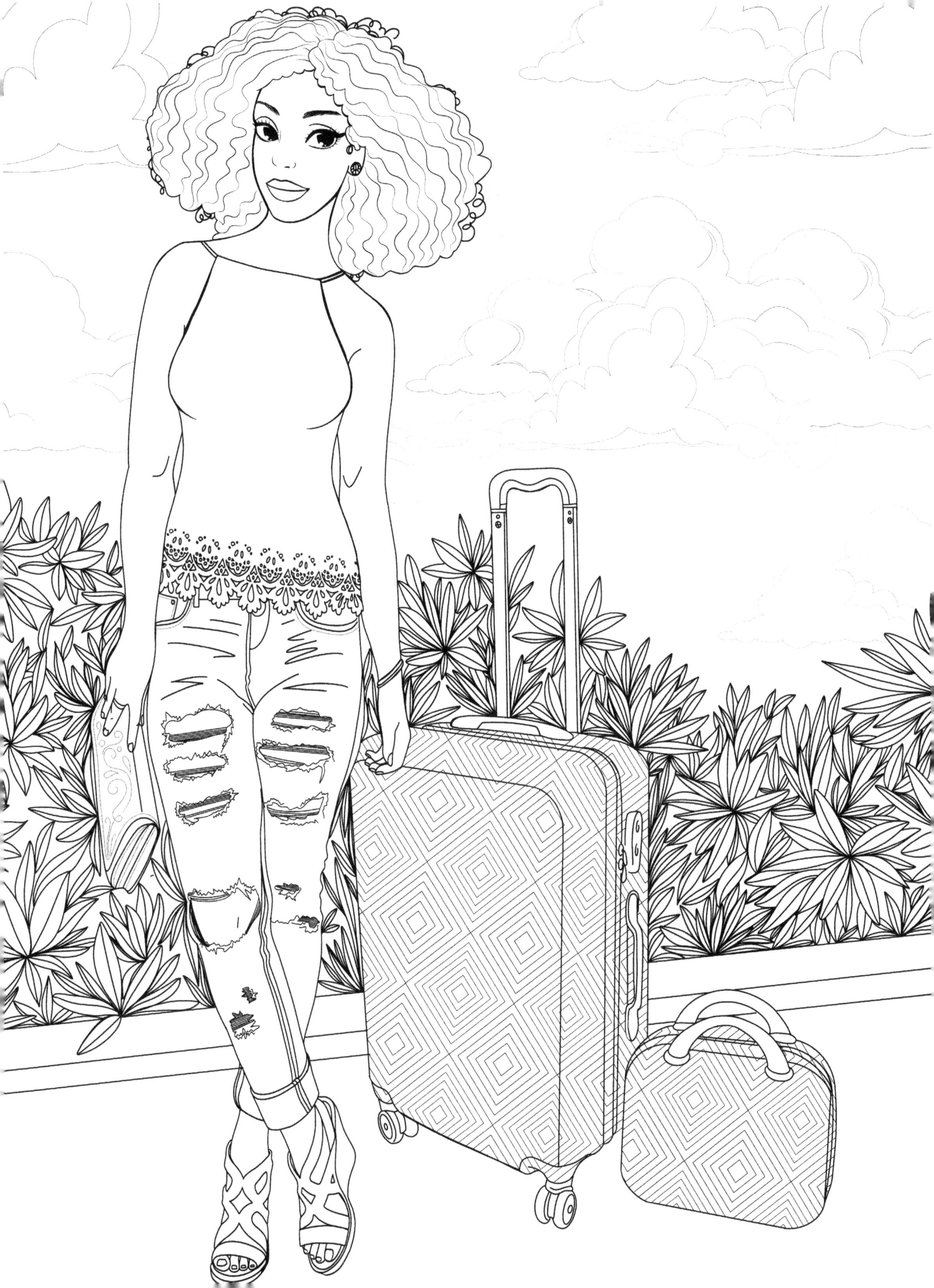

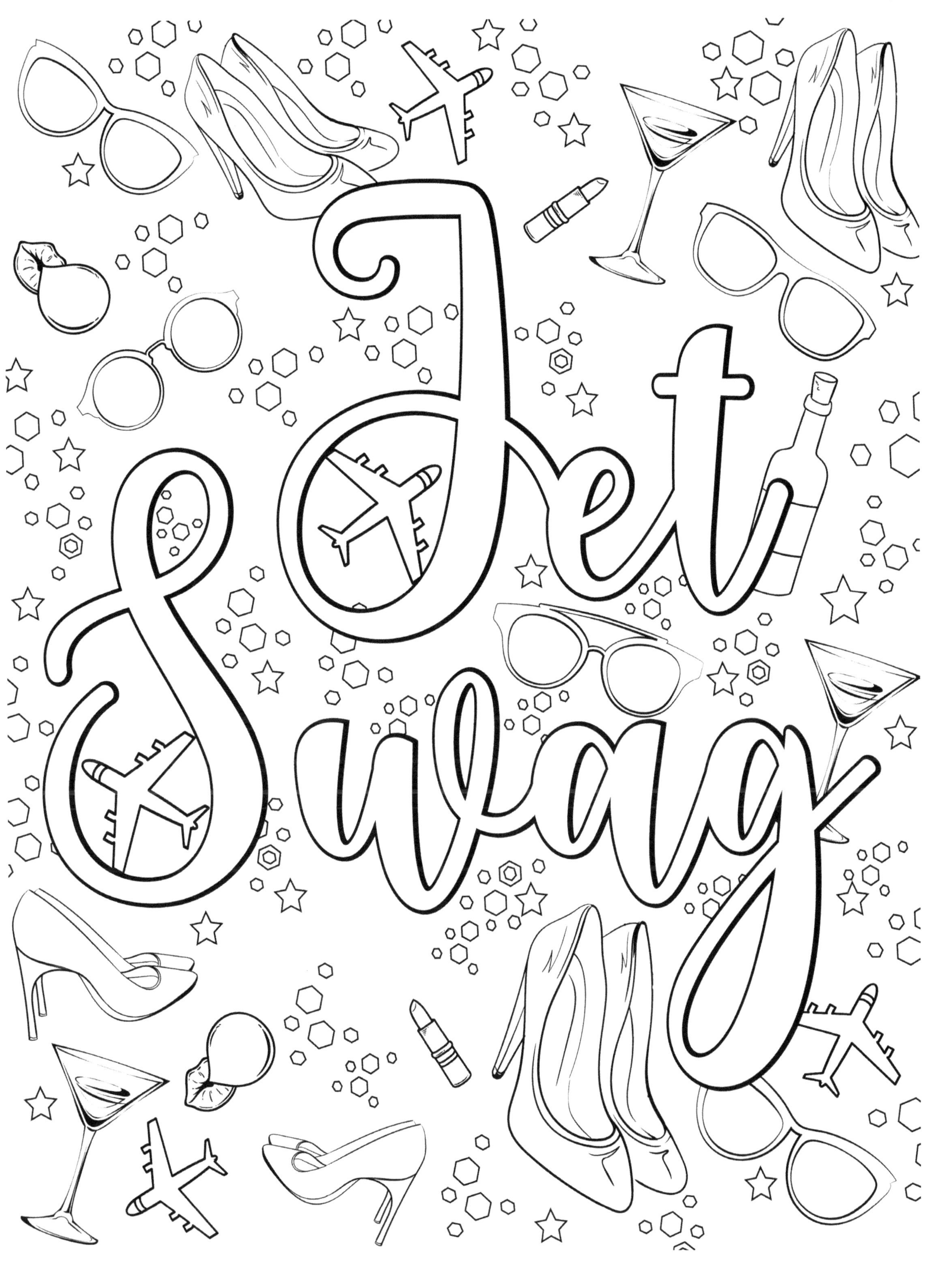
Jet
Swag

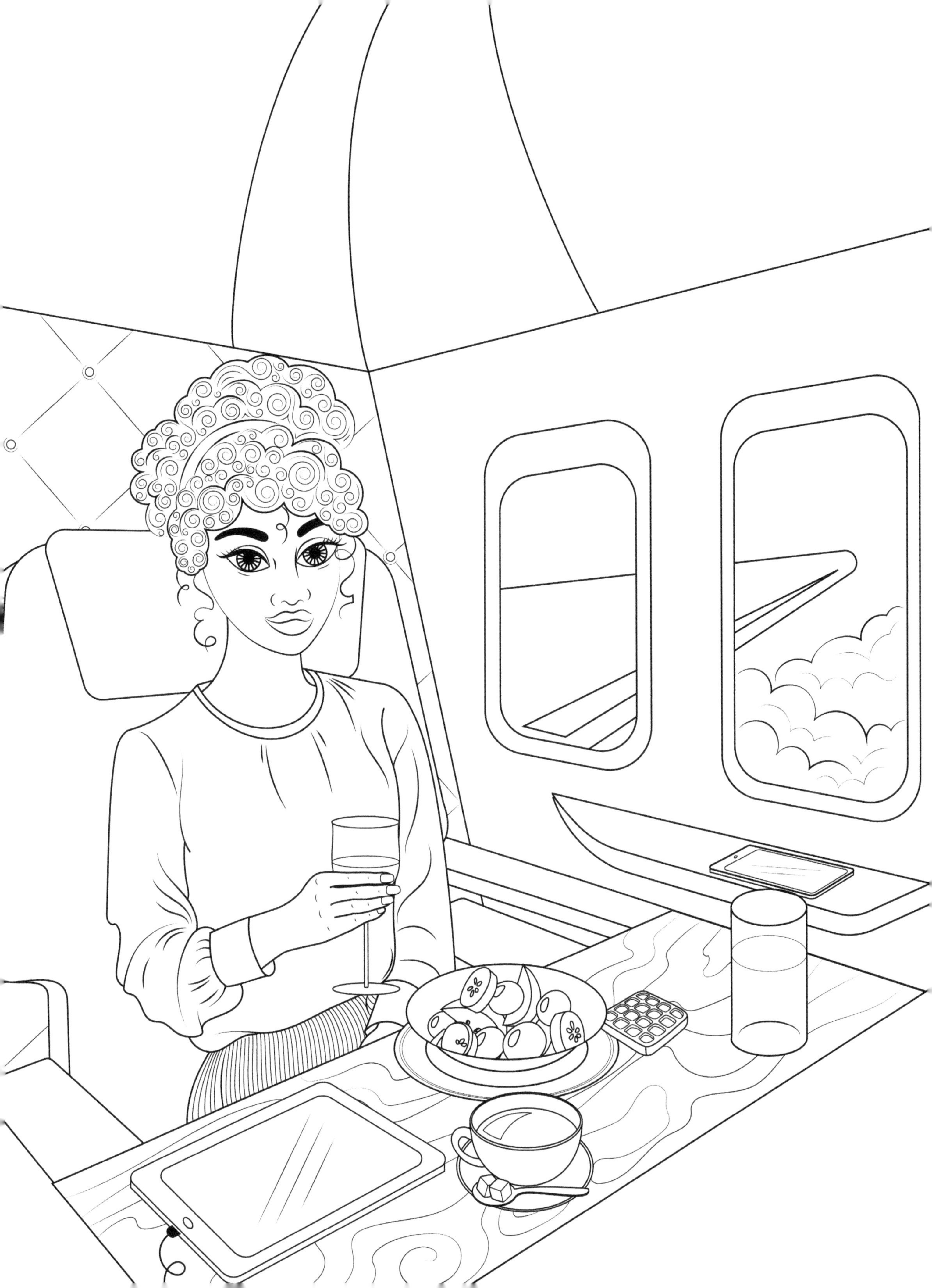

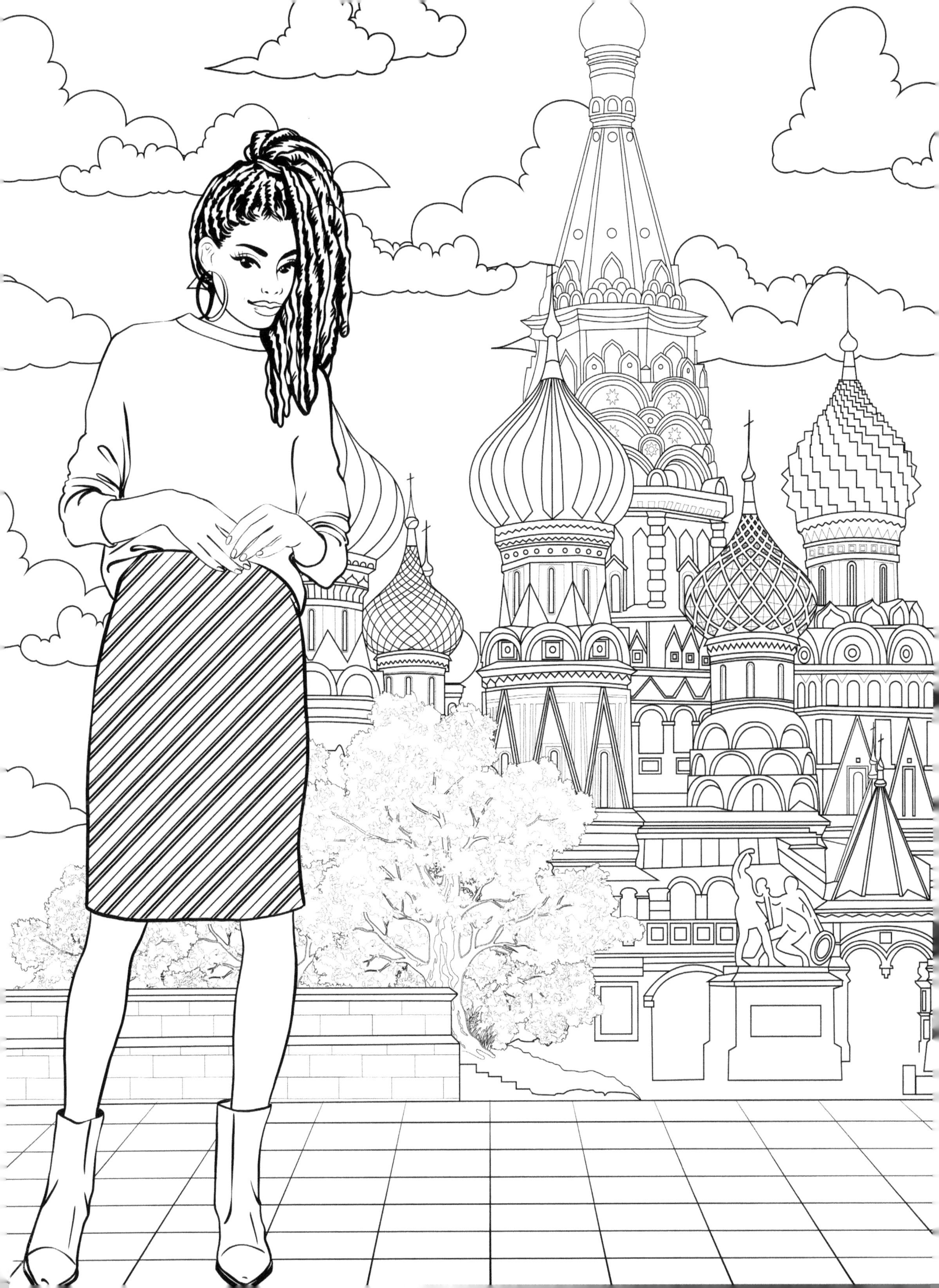

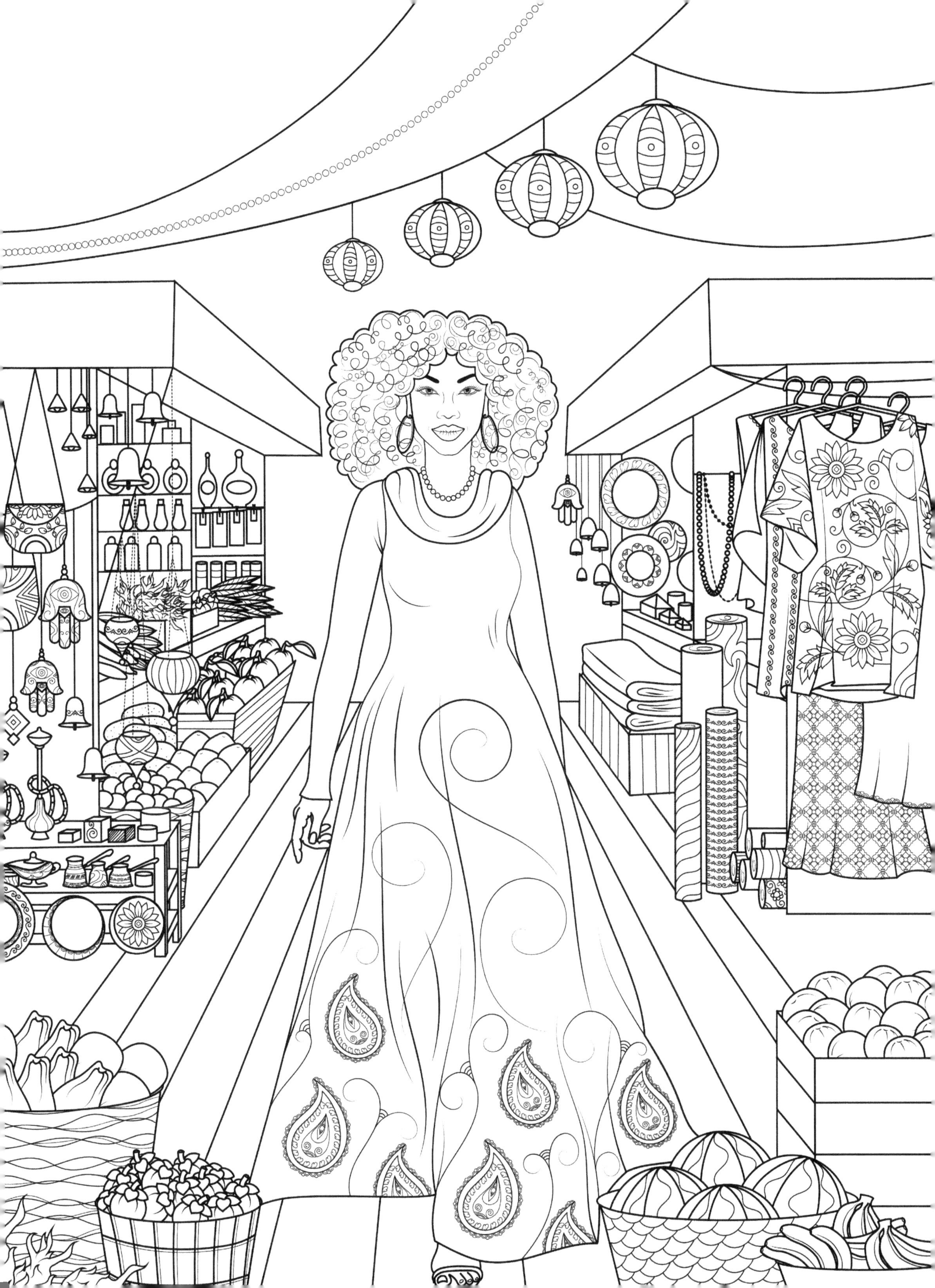

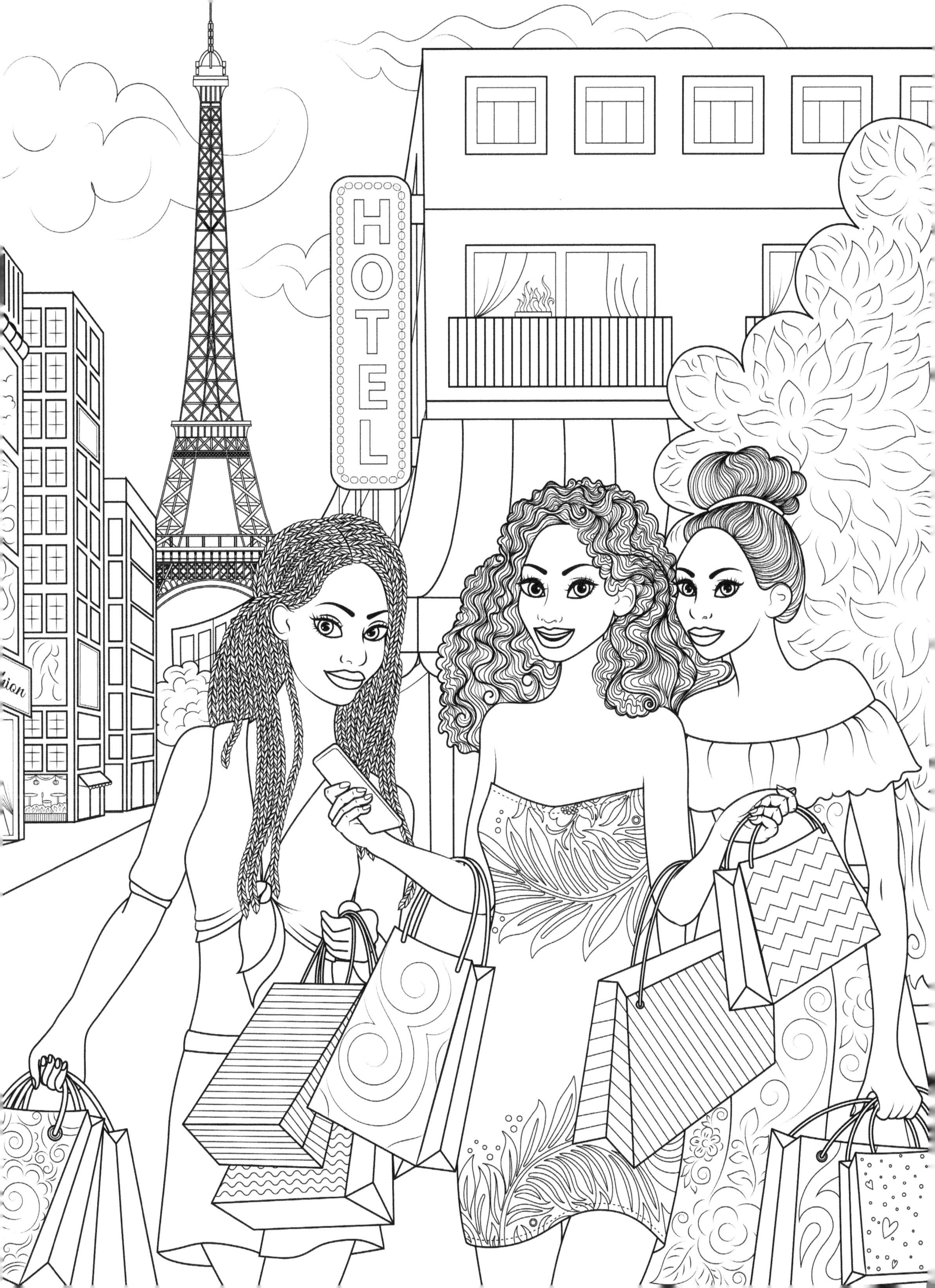
HOTEL

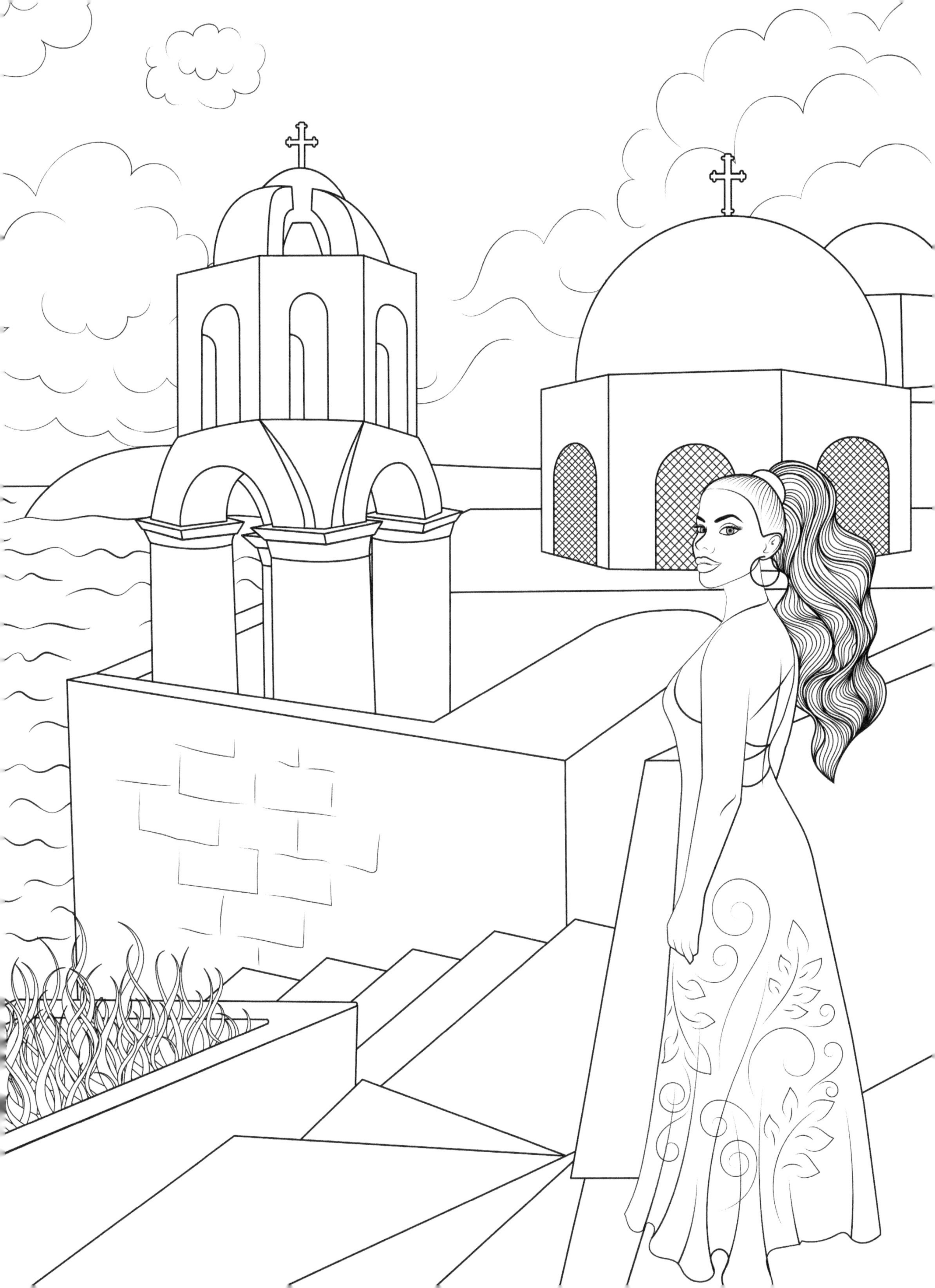

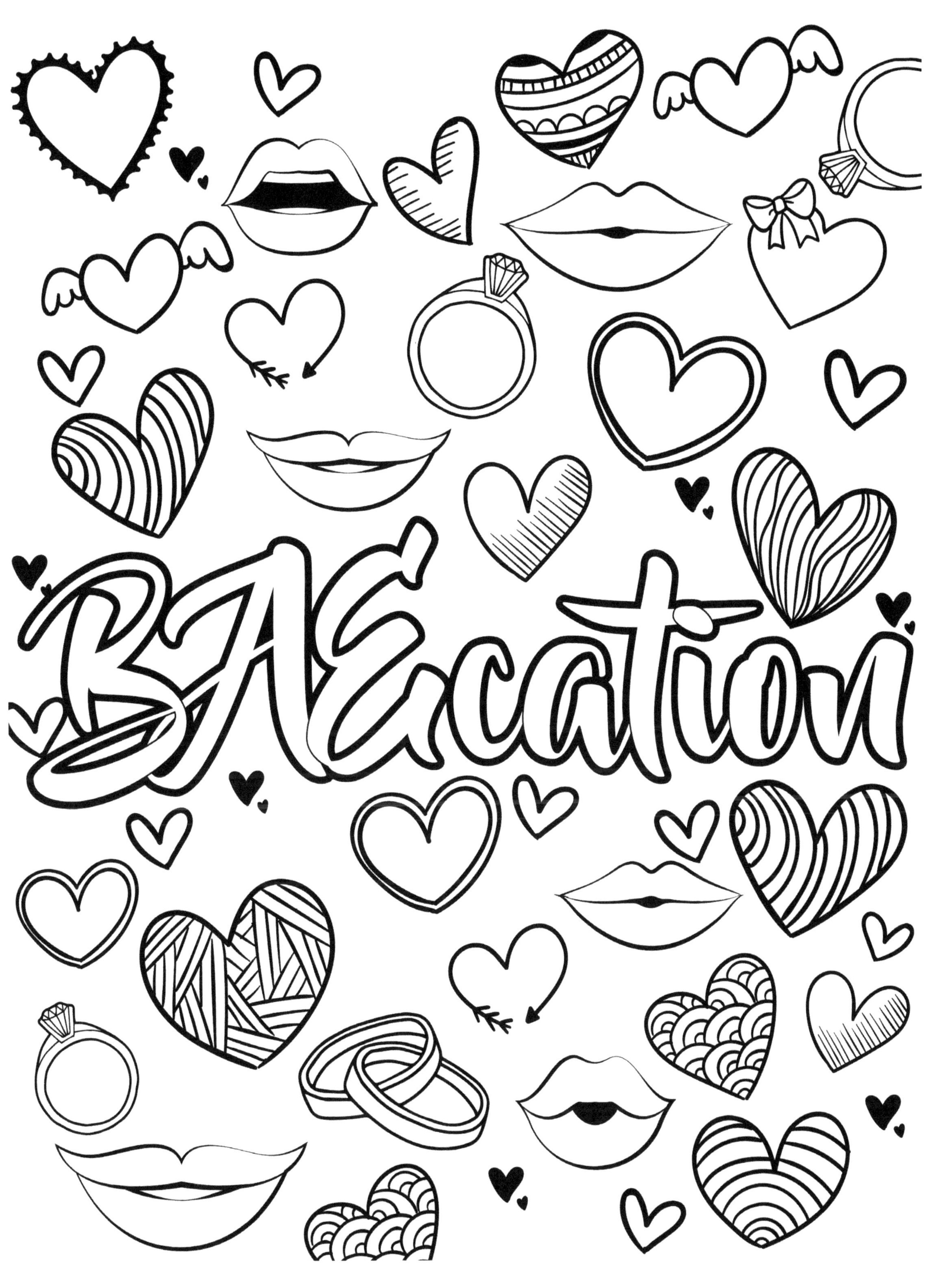
BAEcation

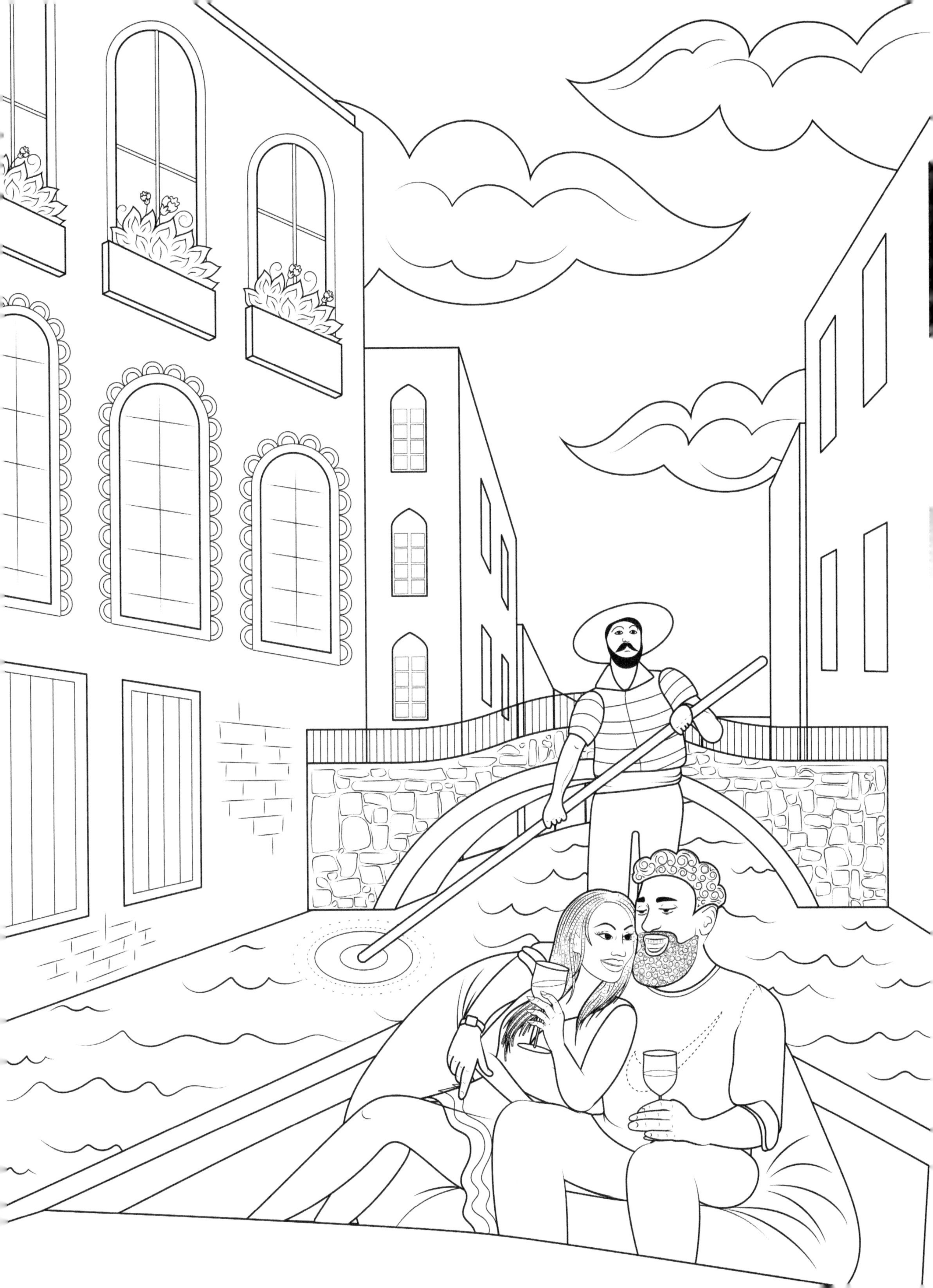

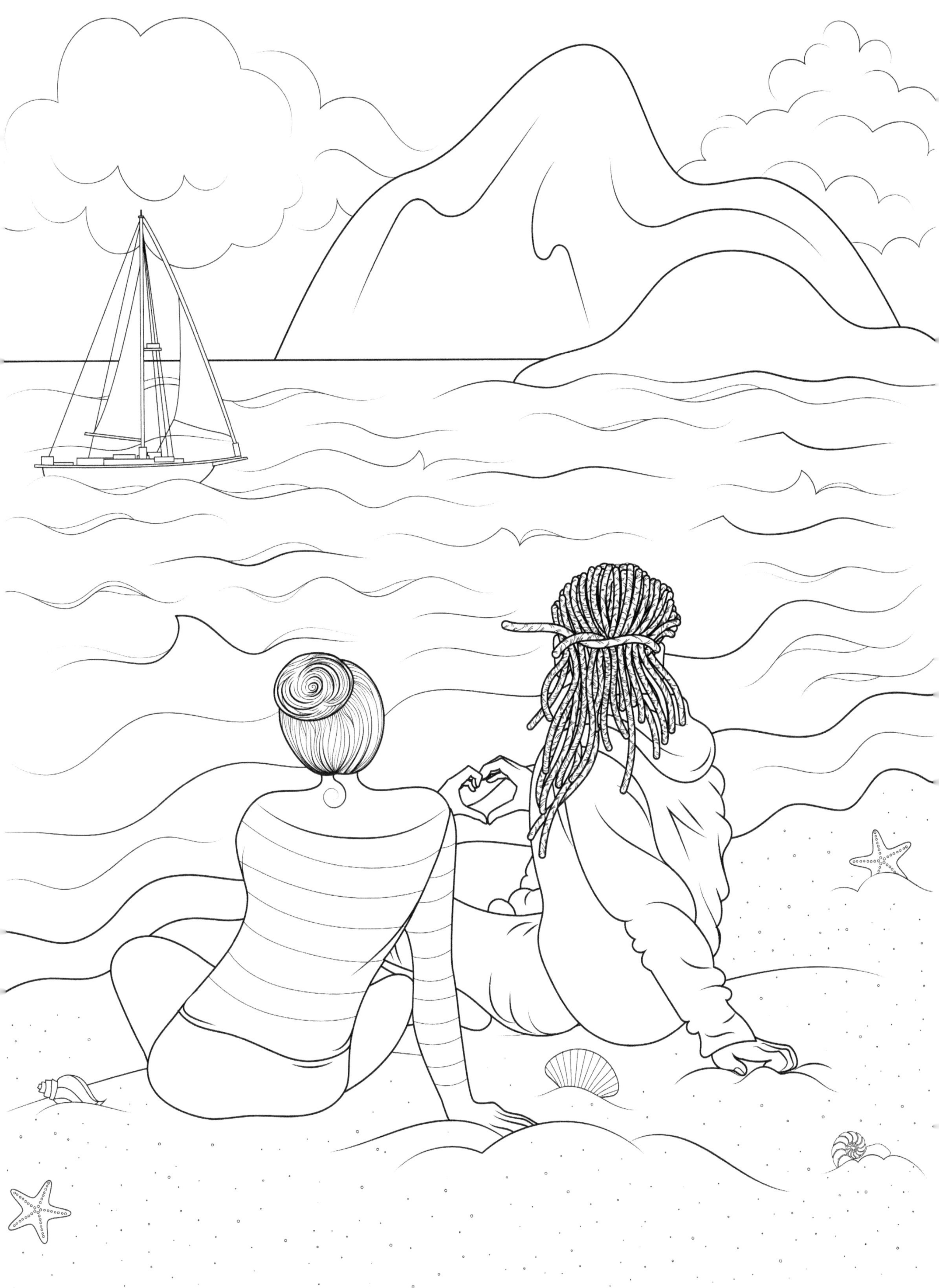

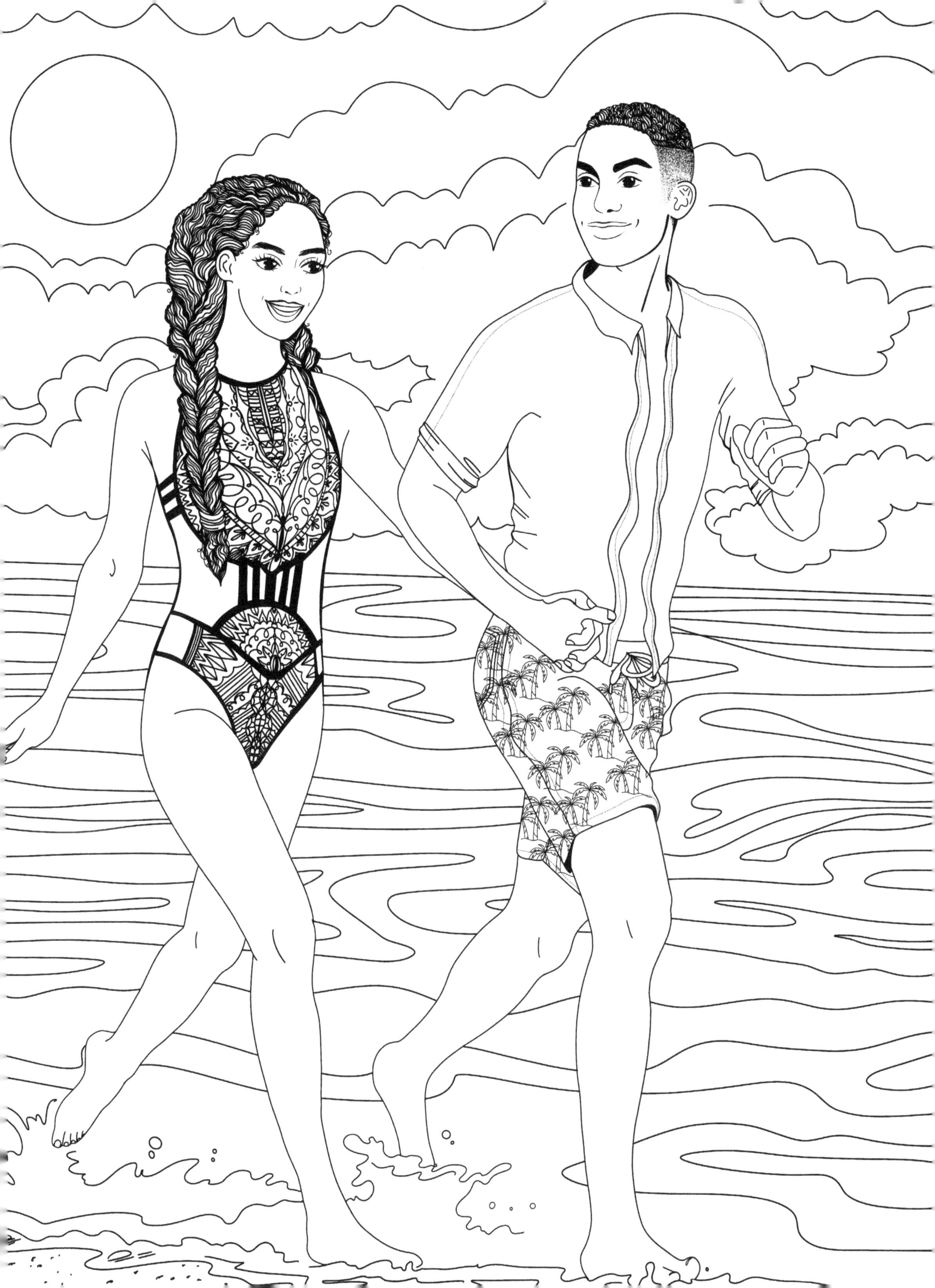

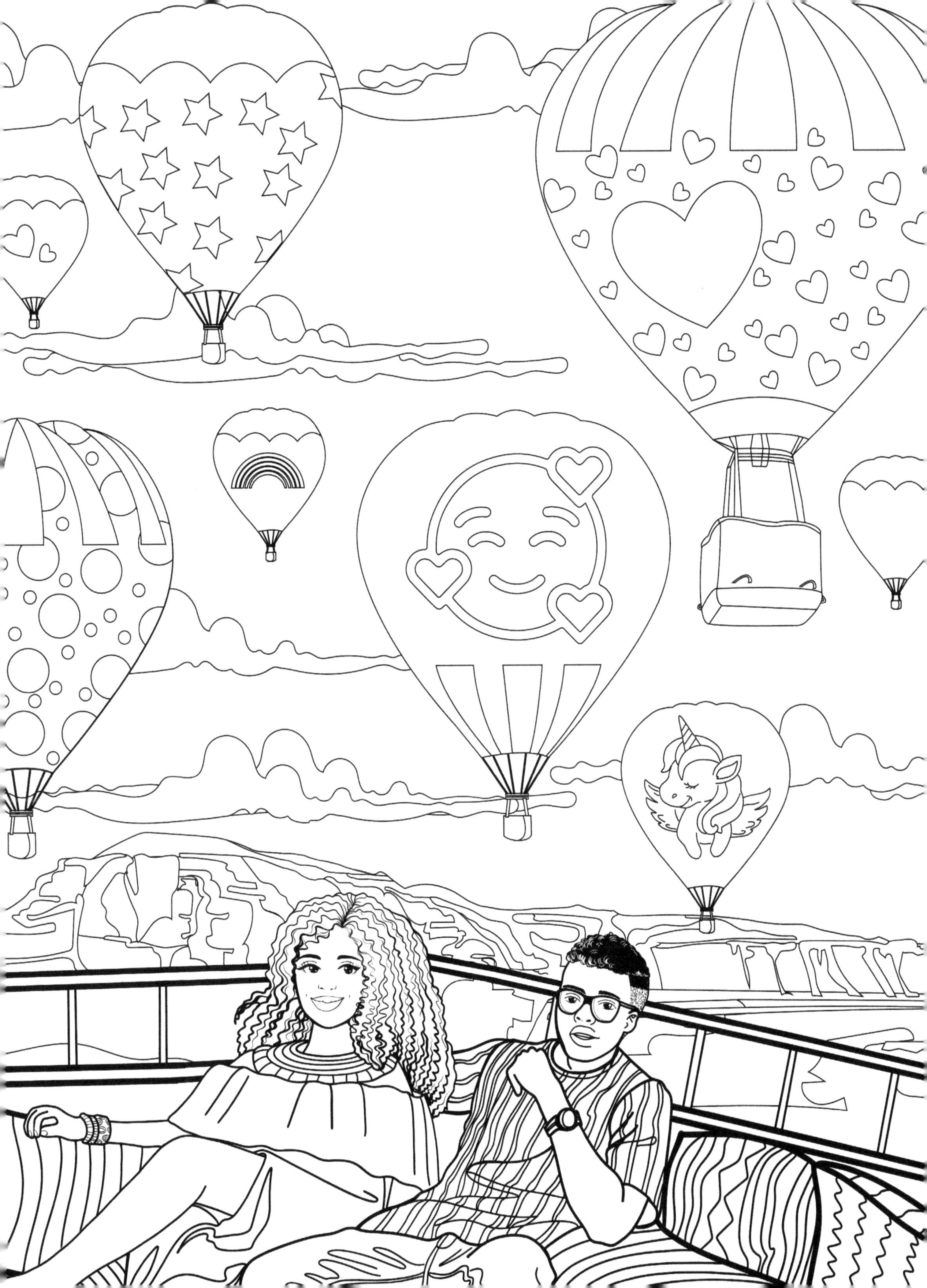

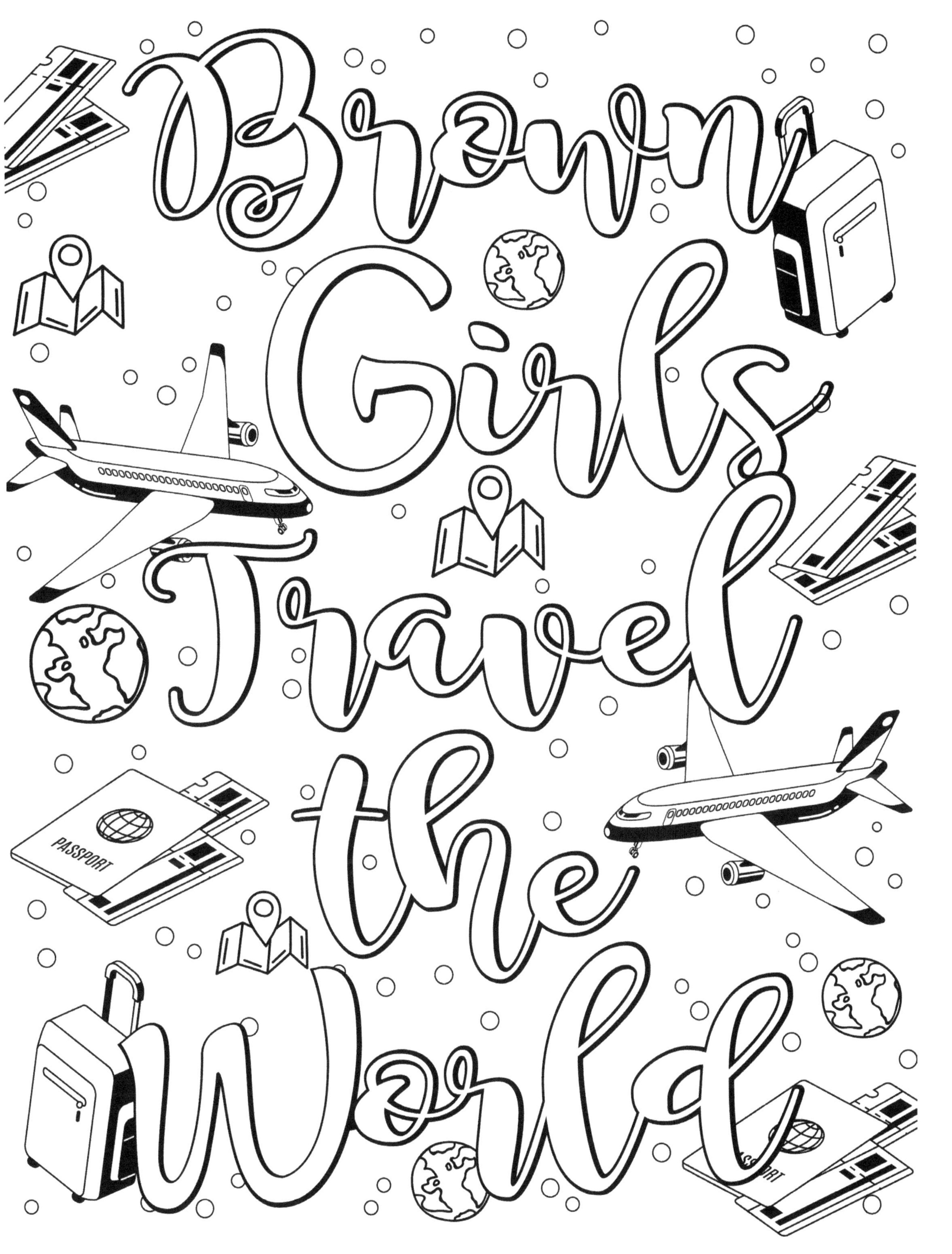
Brown
Girls
Travel
the
World
PASSPORT

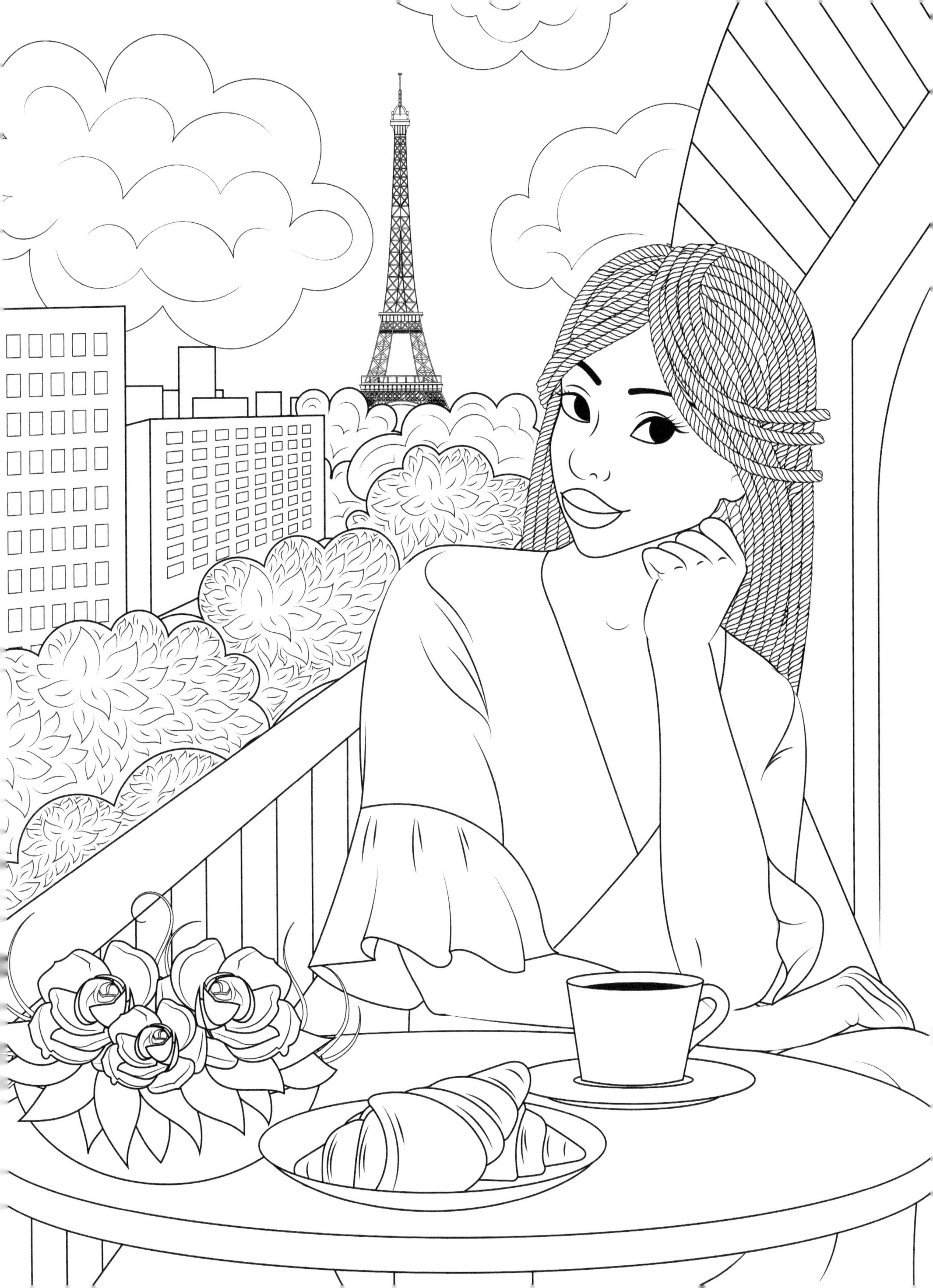

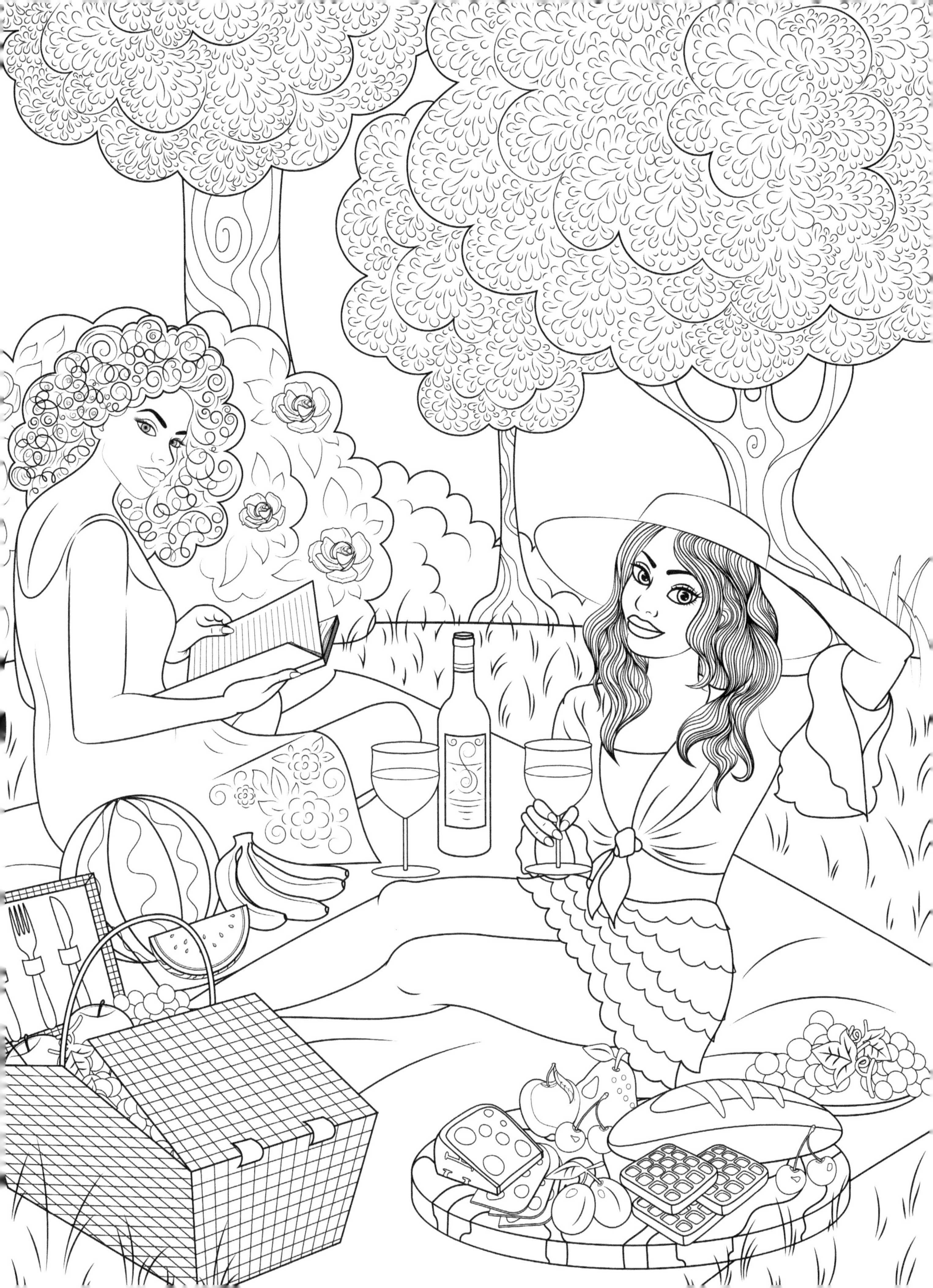

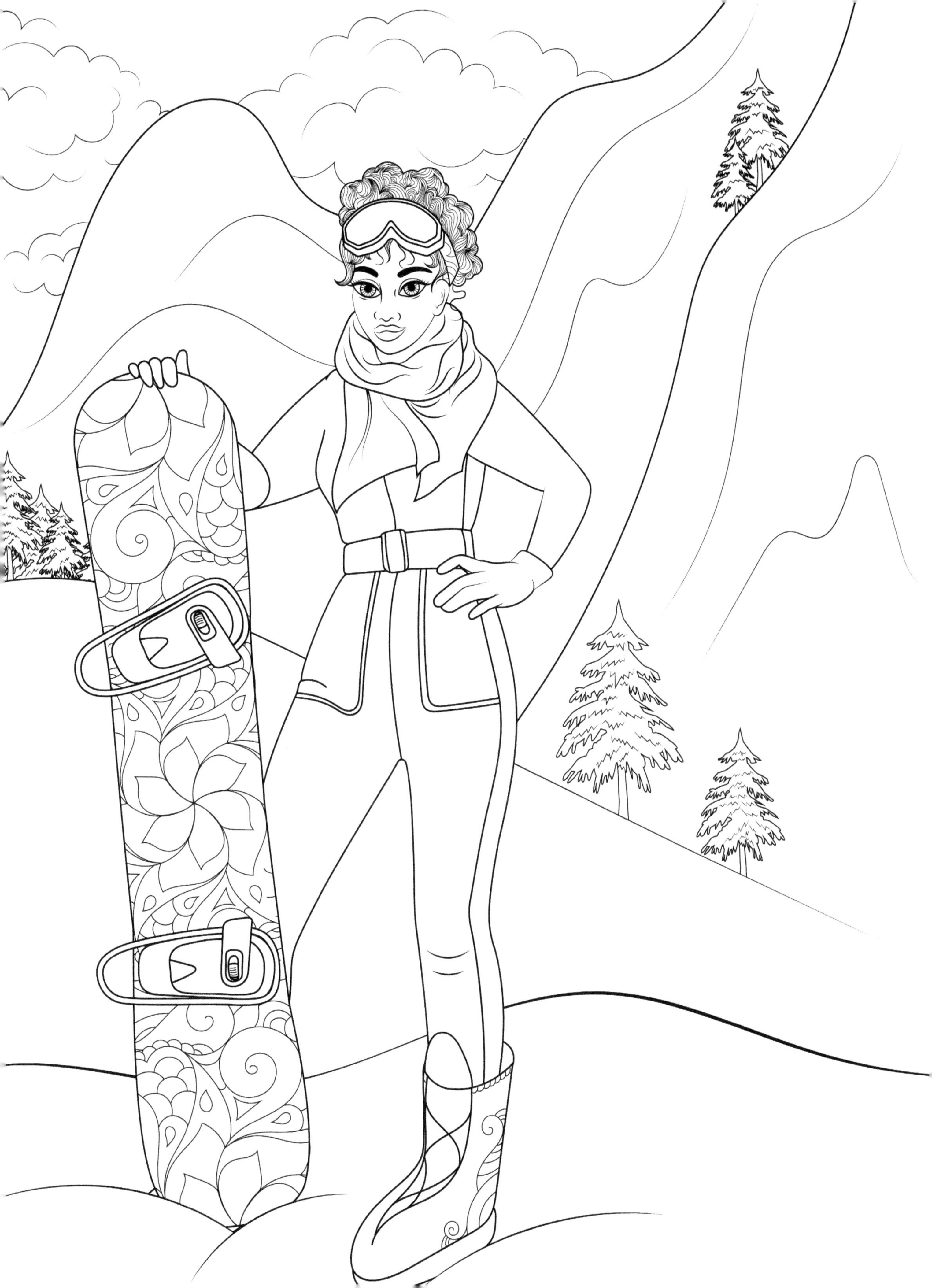

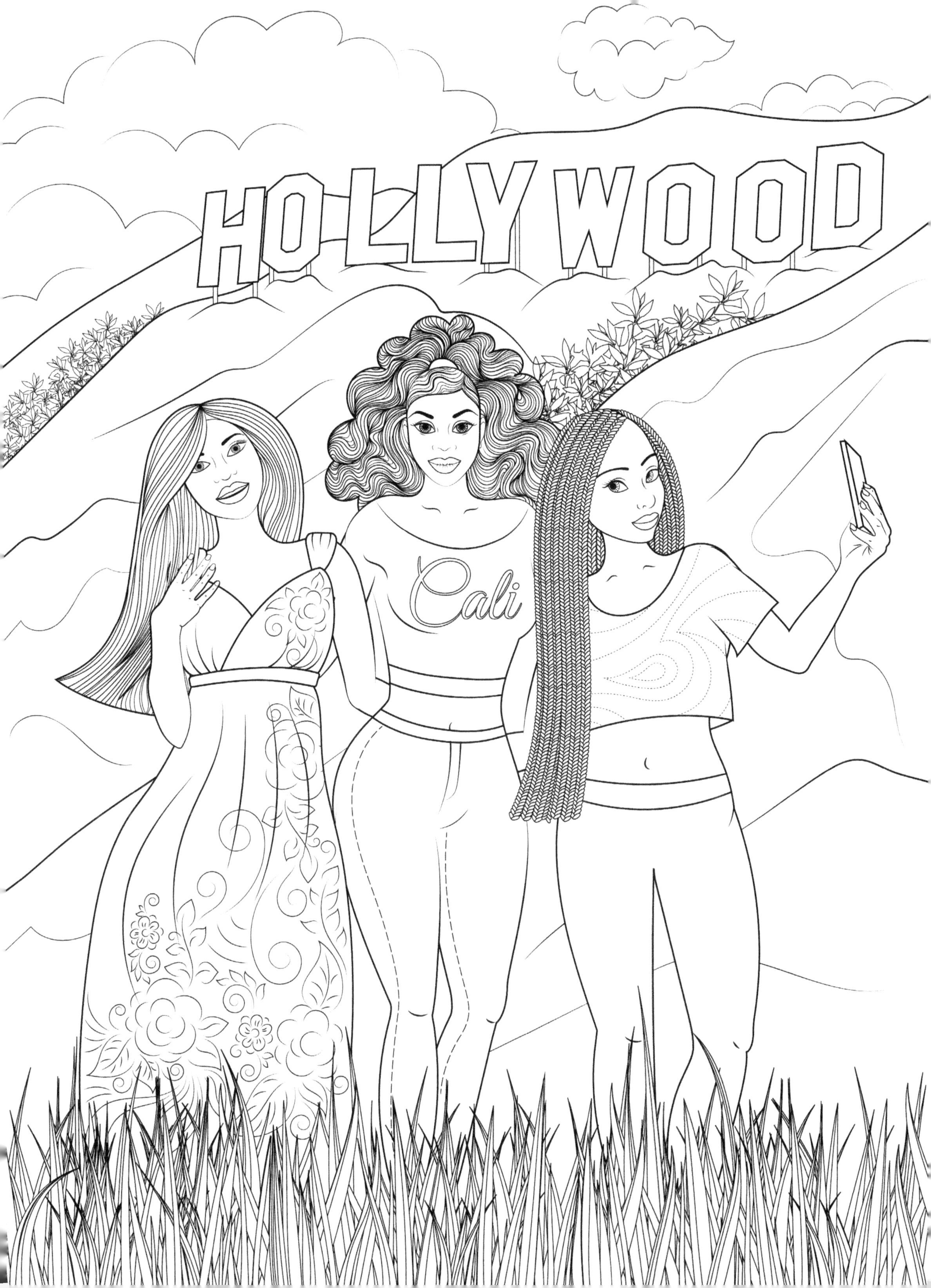
HOLLYWOOD
Cali

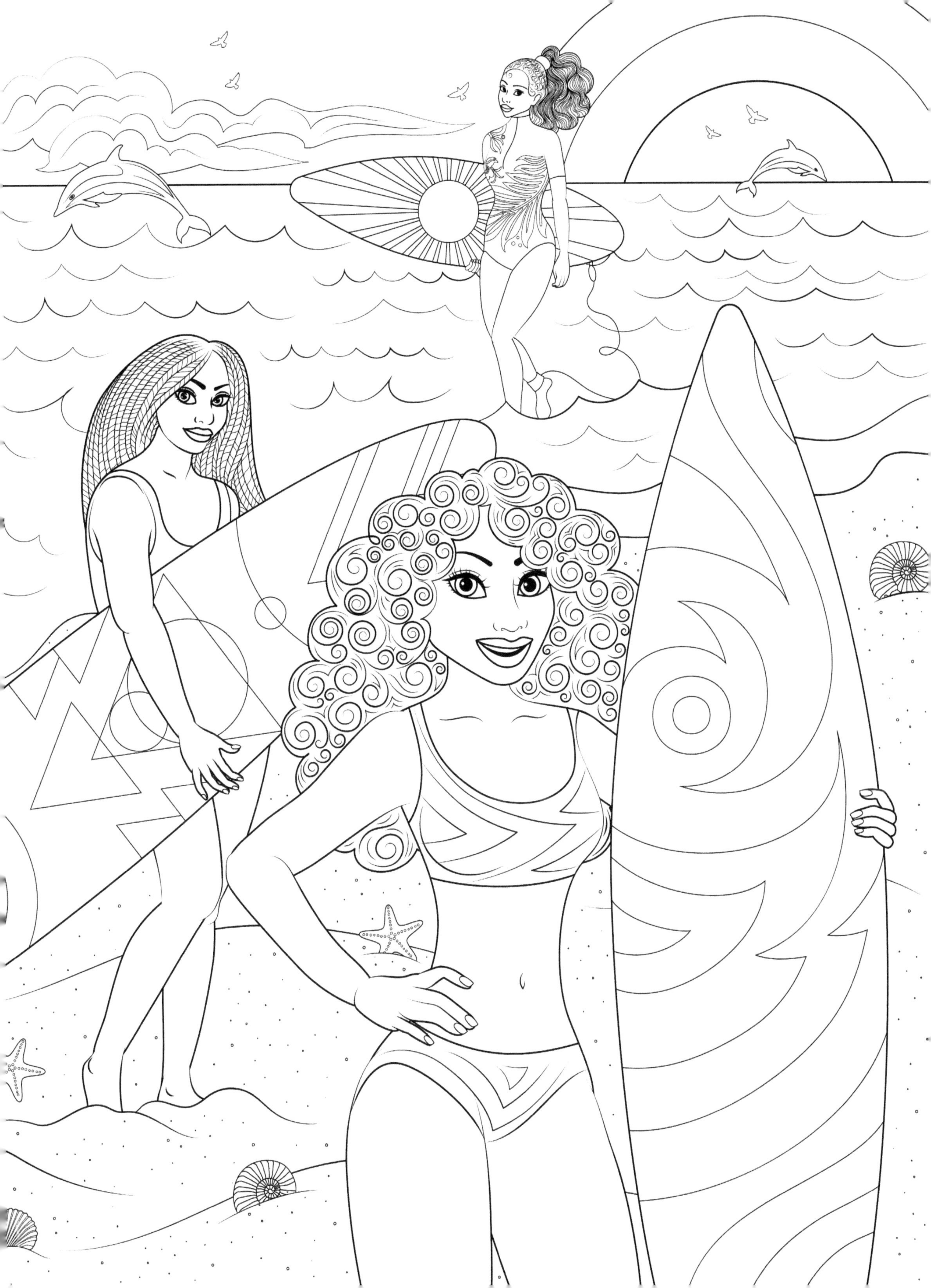

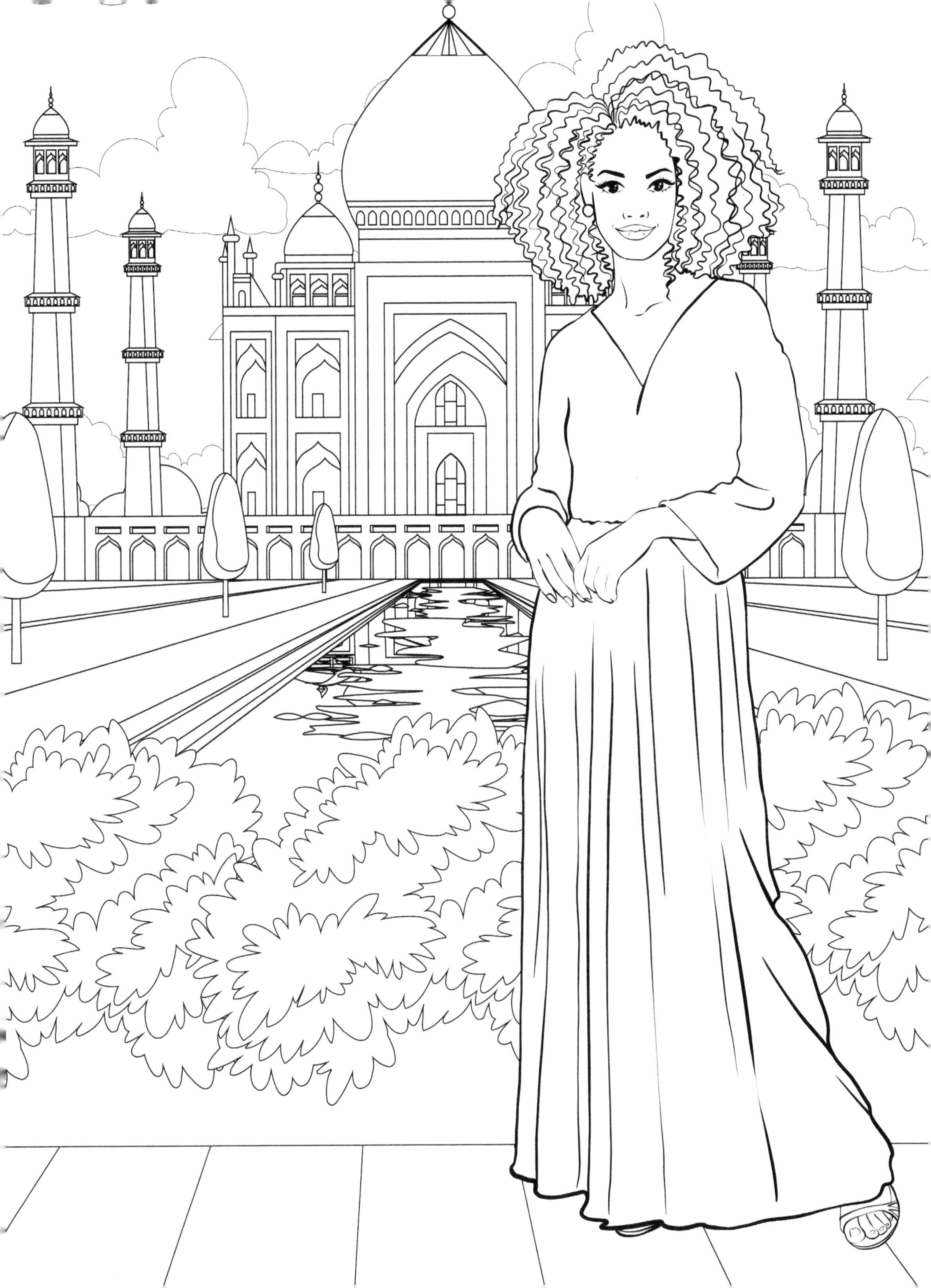

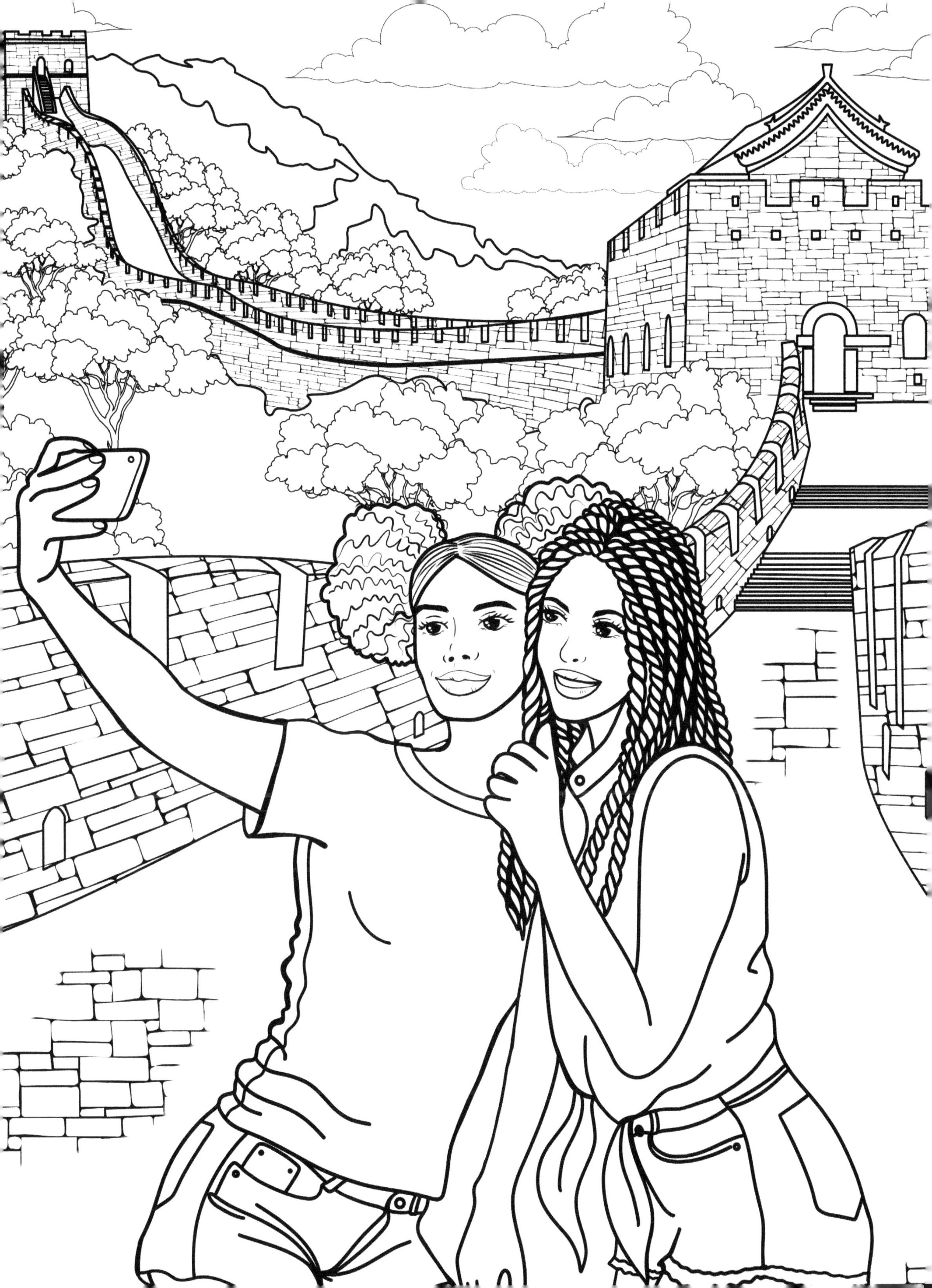

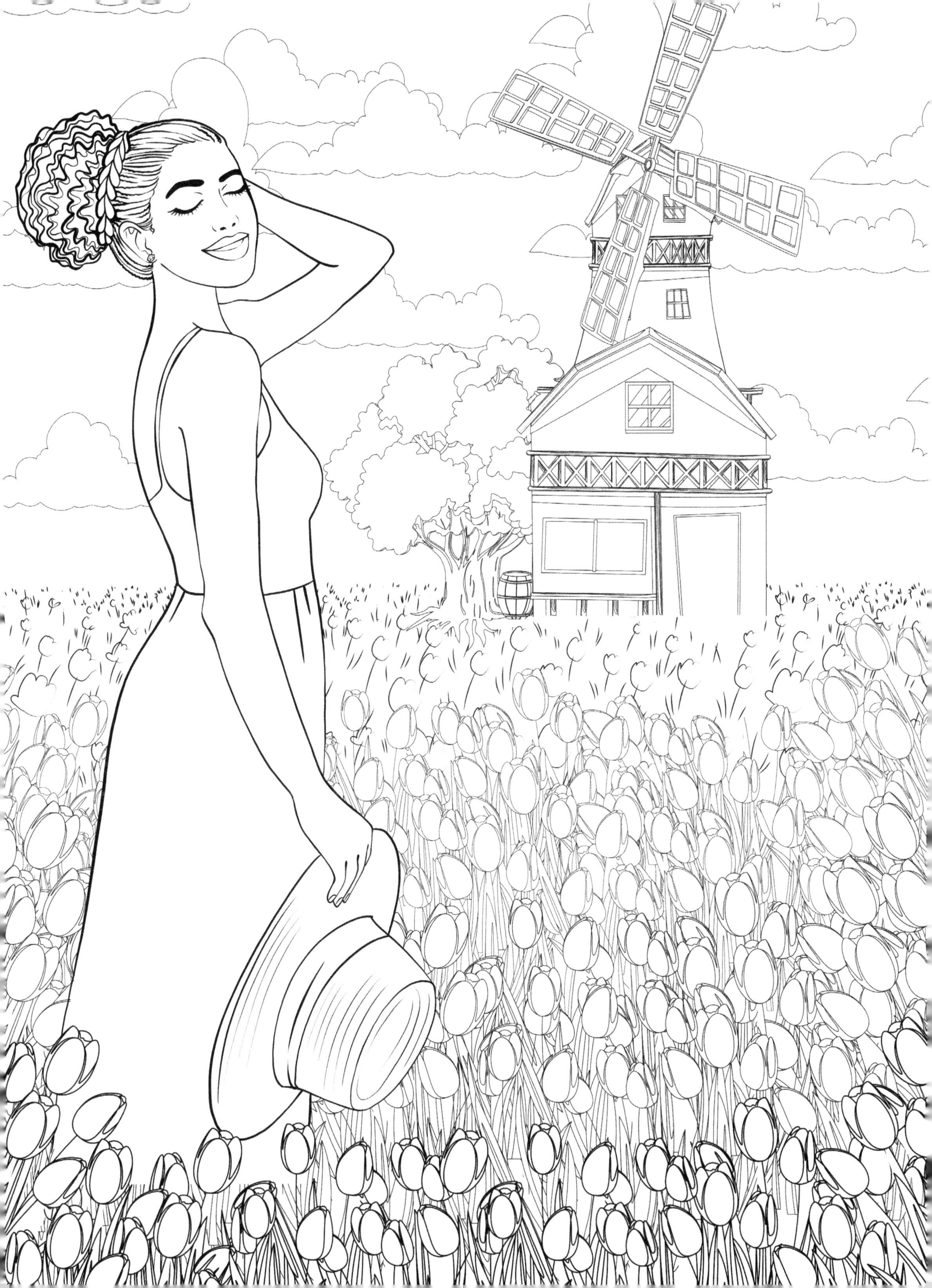

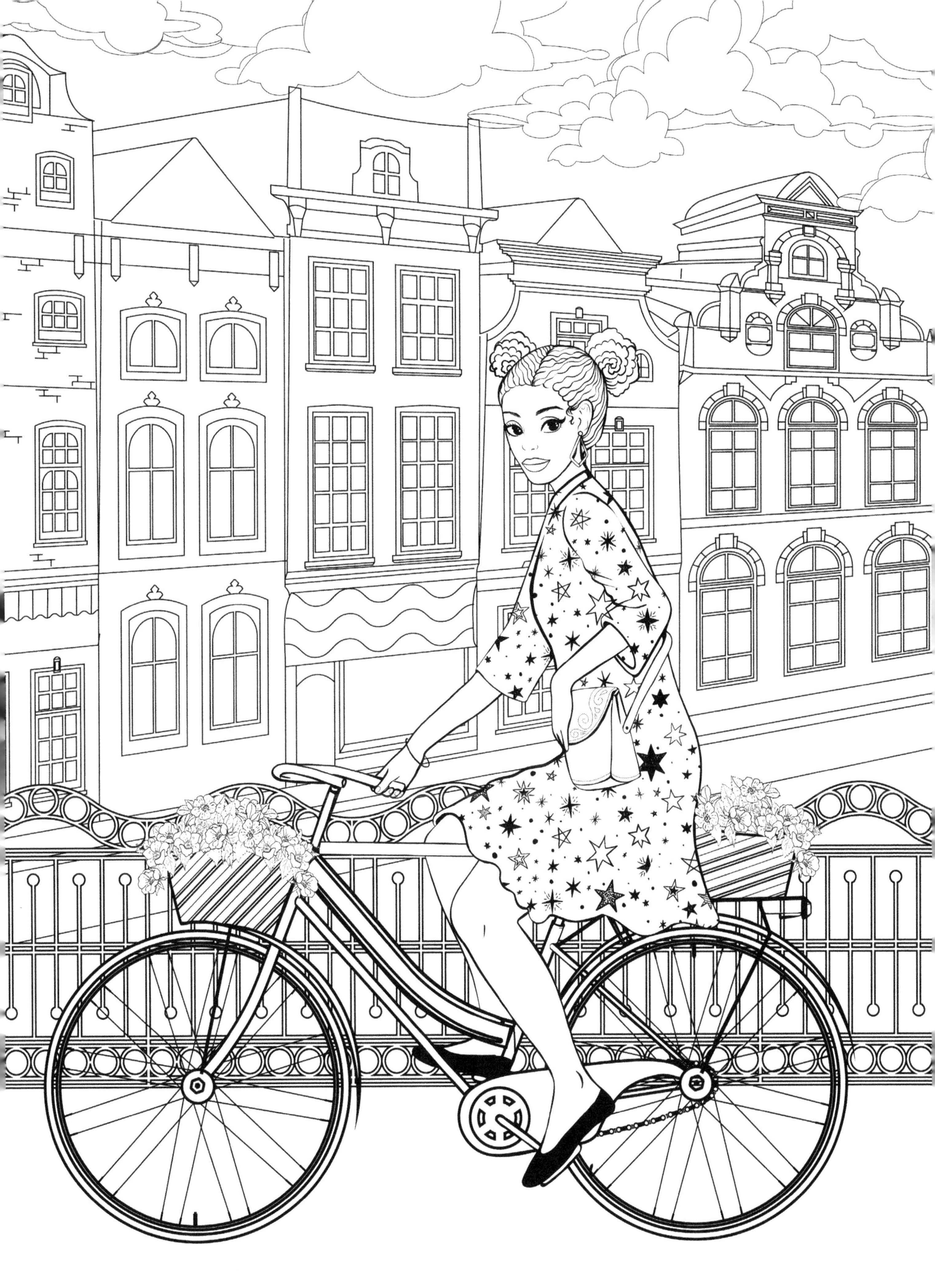

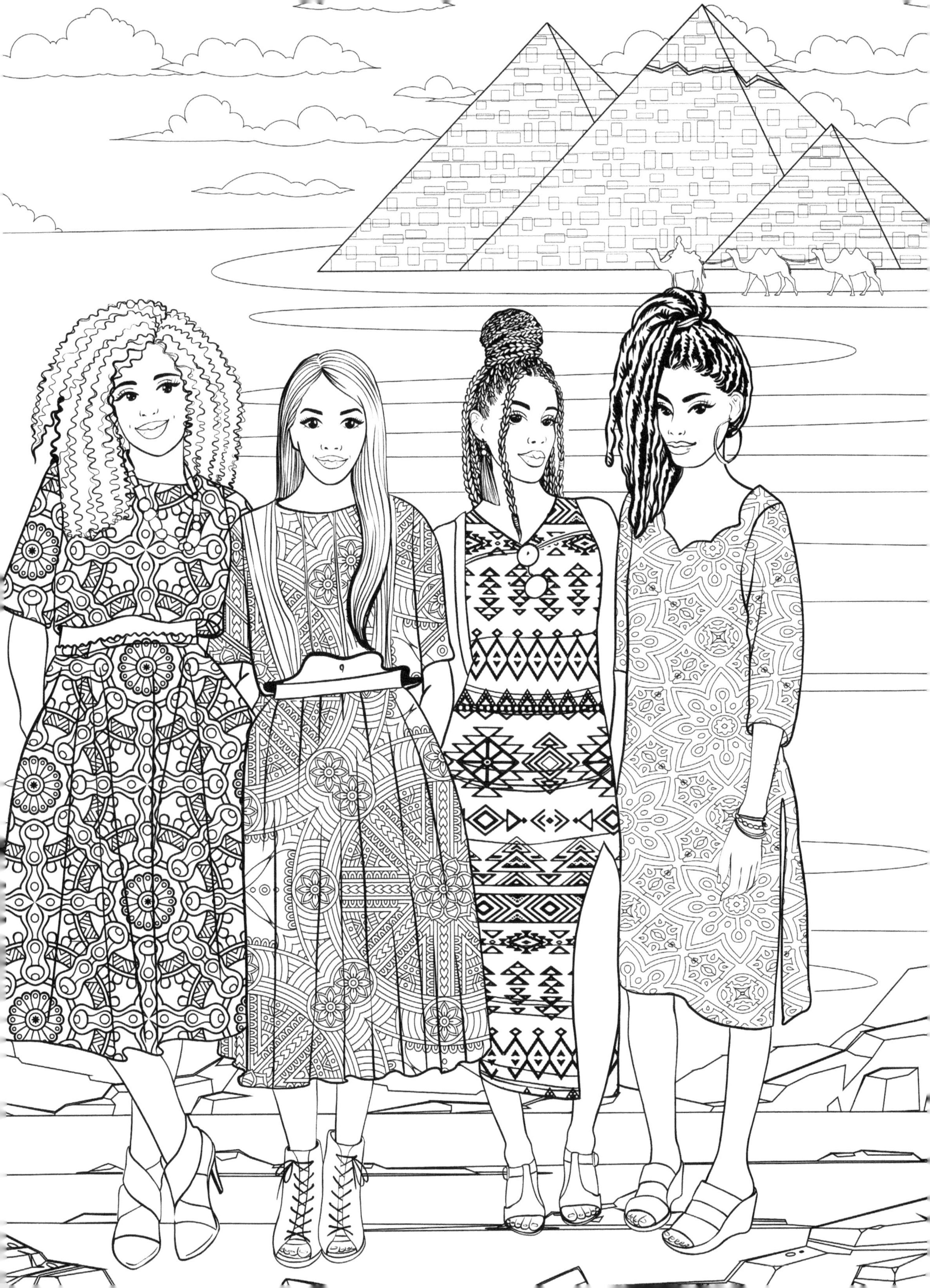

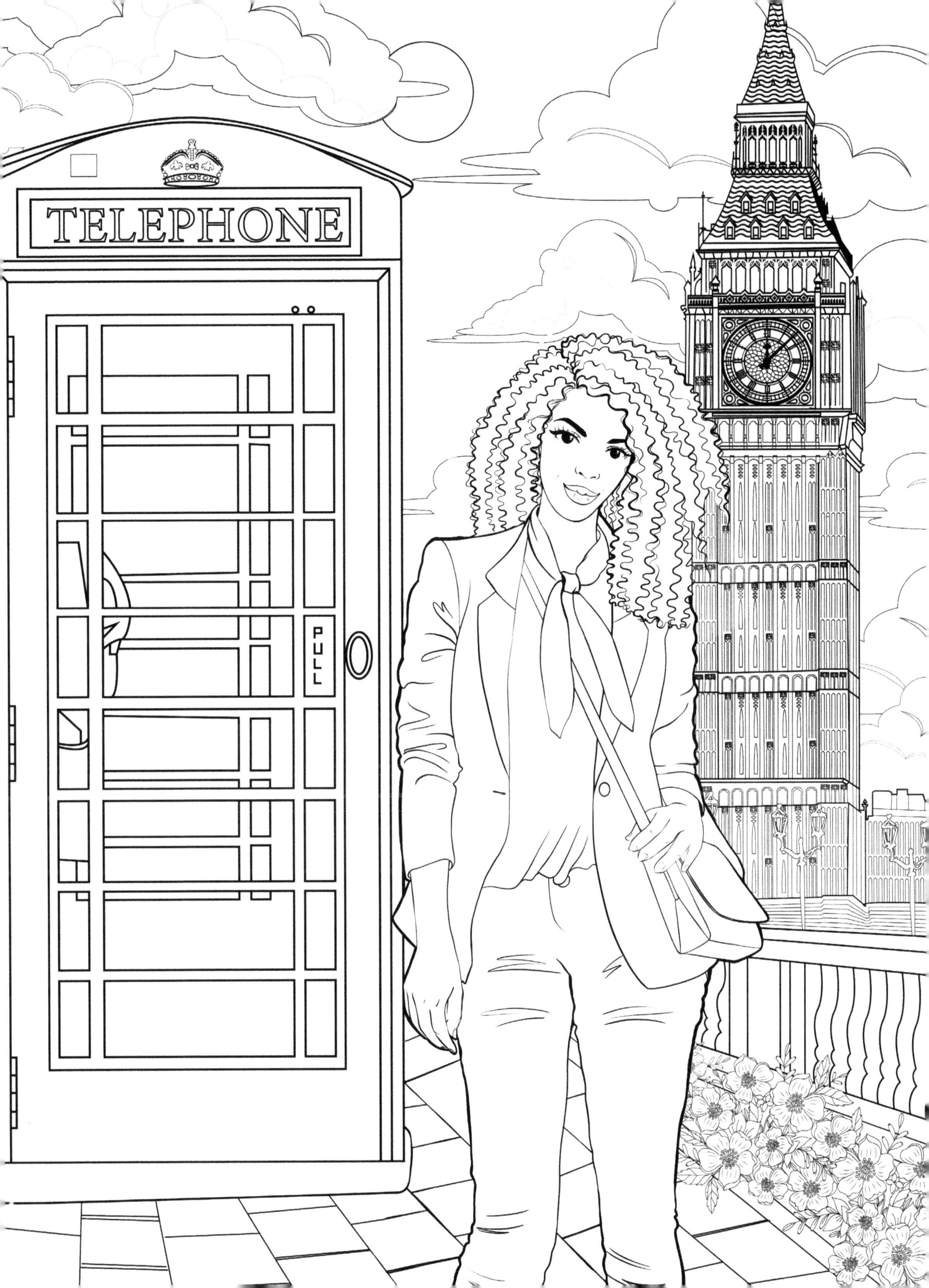
TELEPHONE
PULL

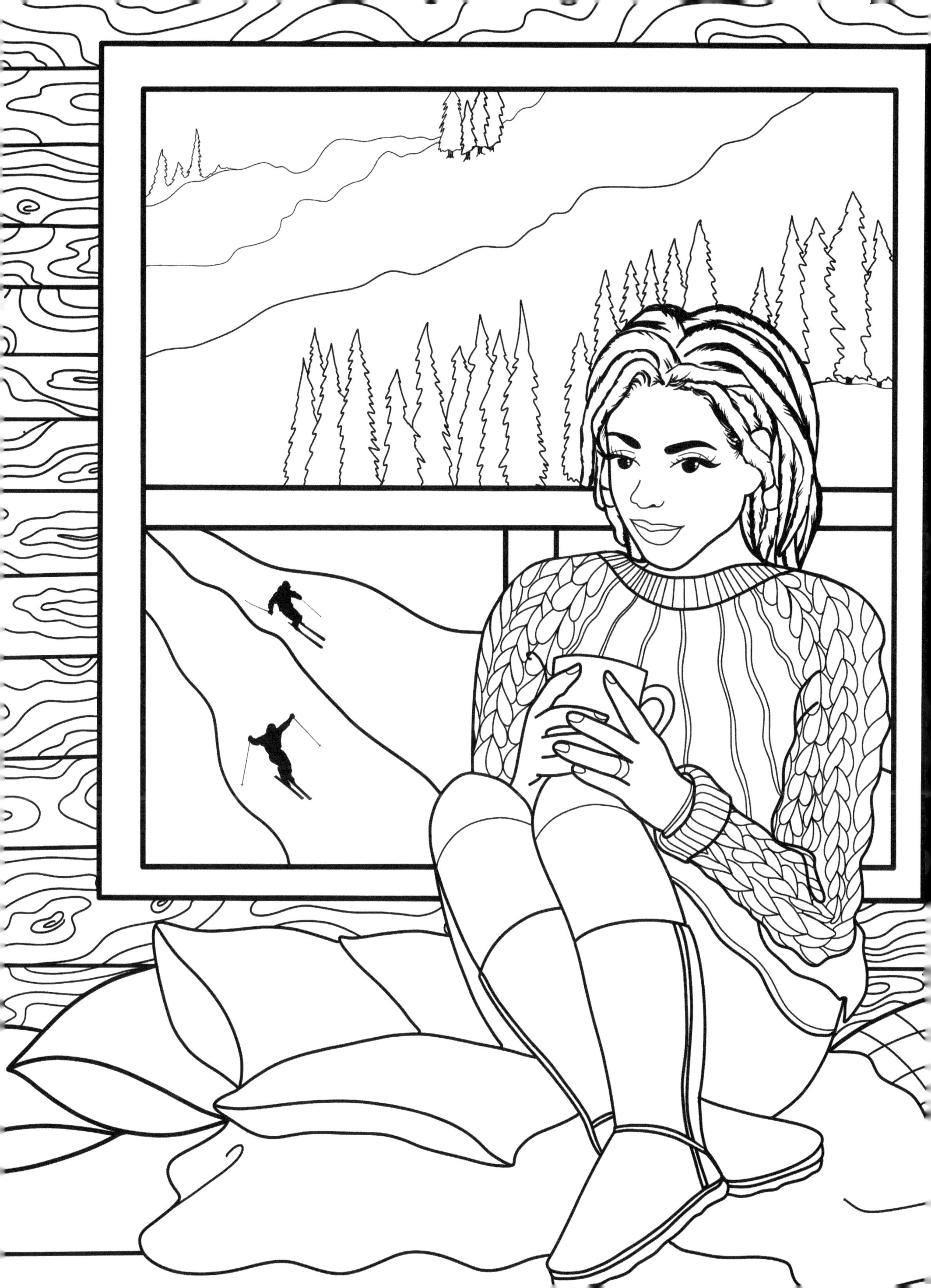

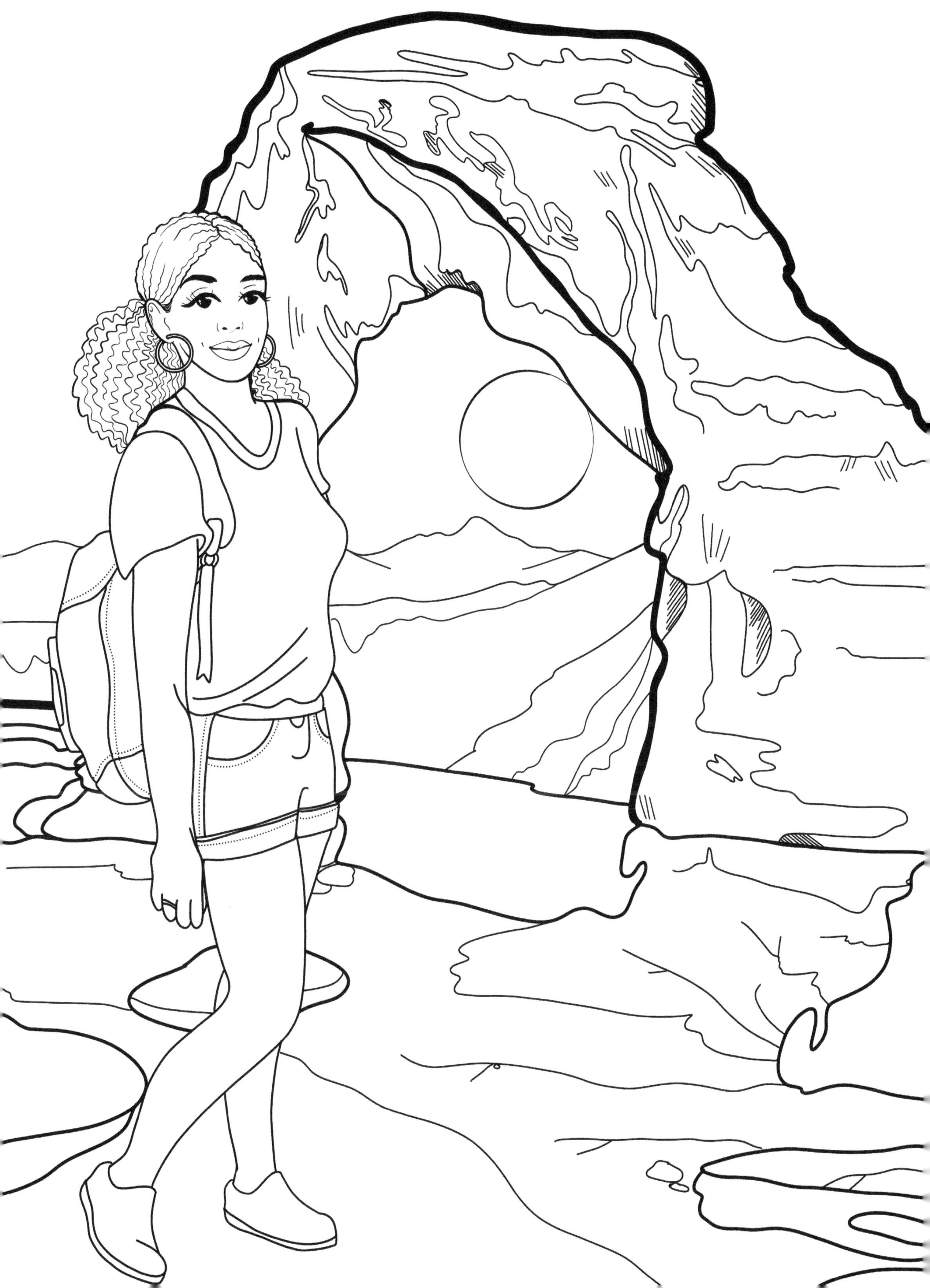

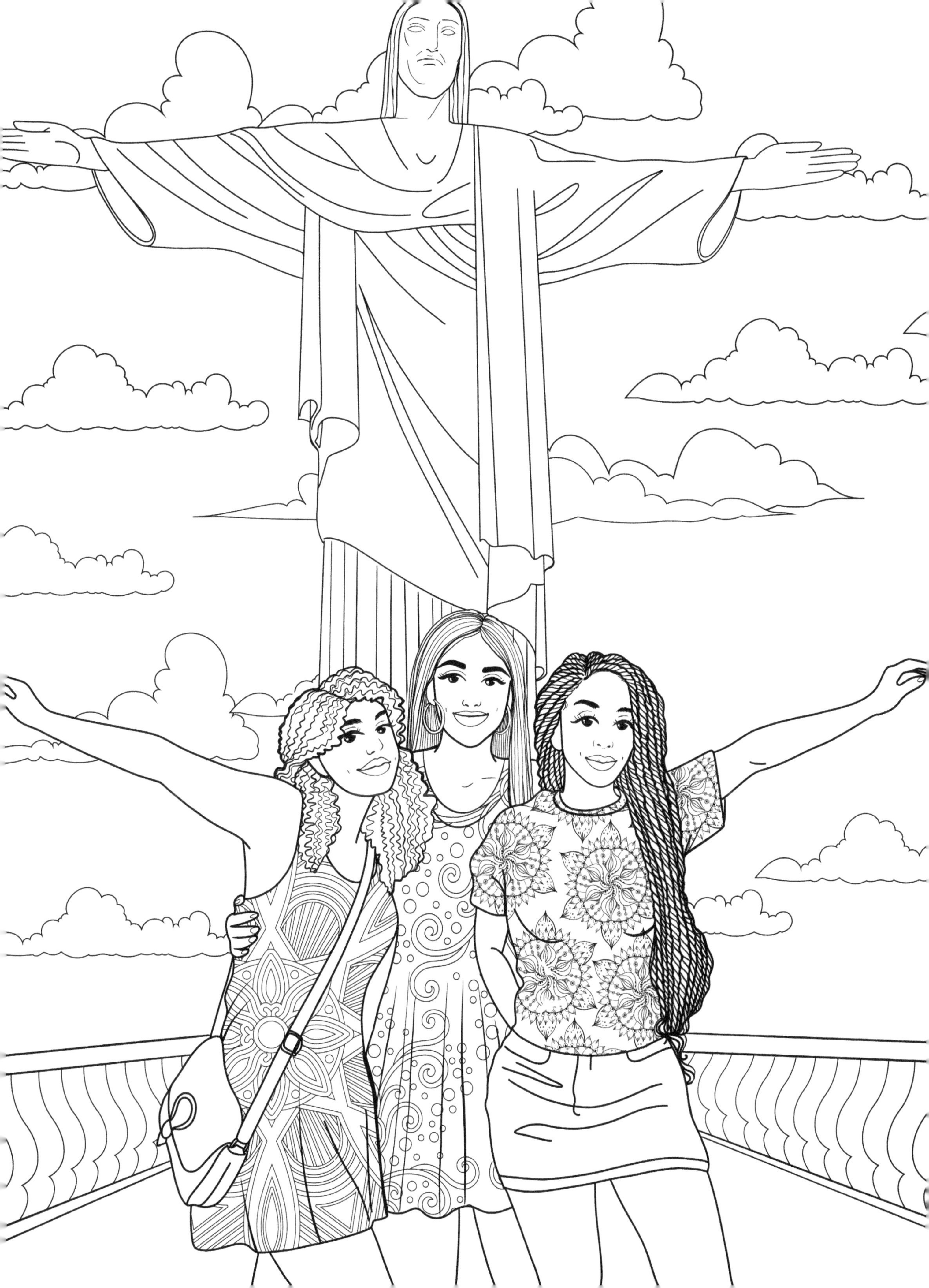

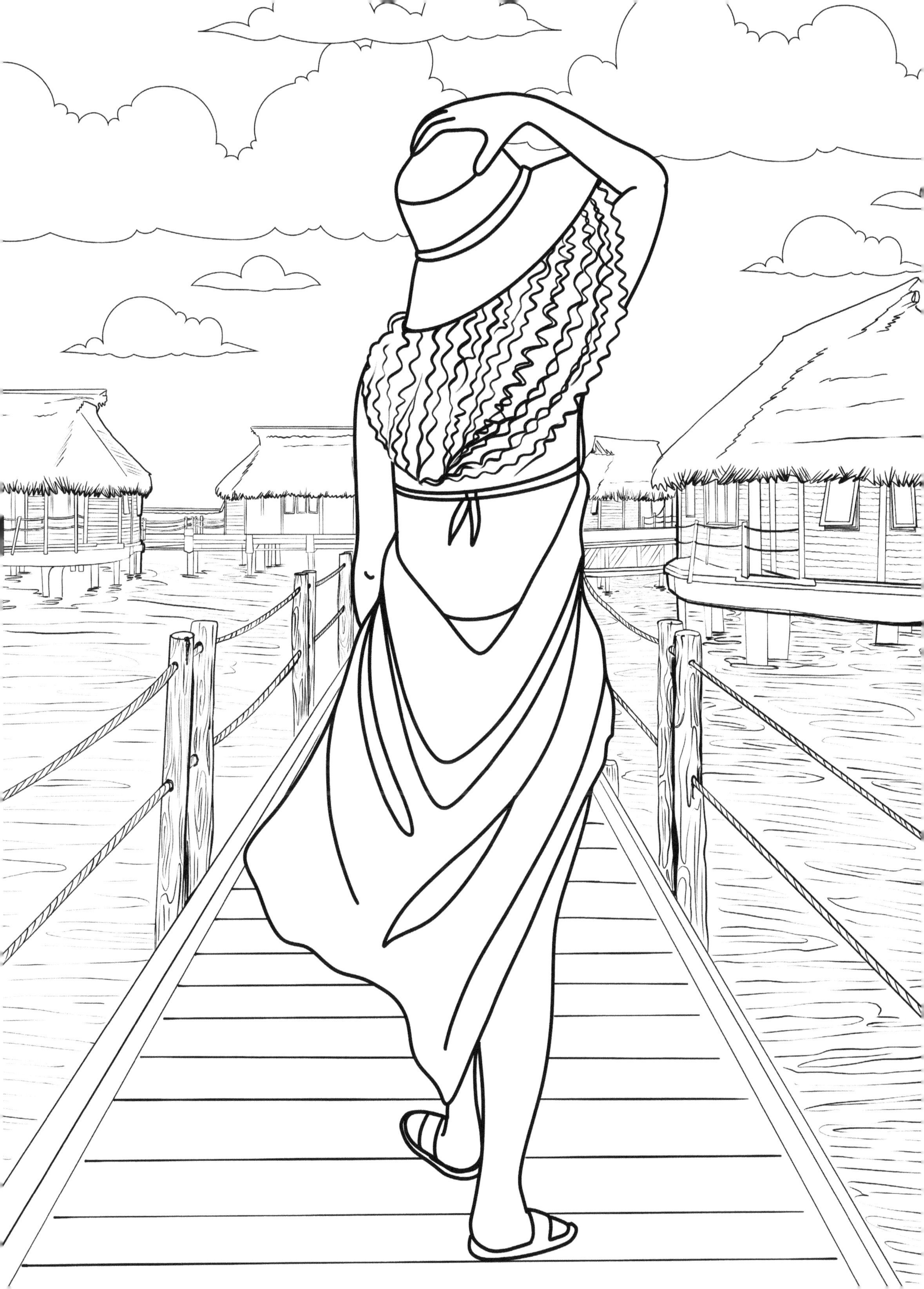

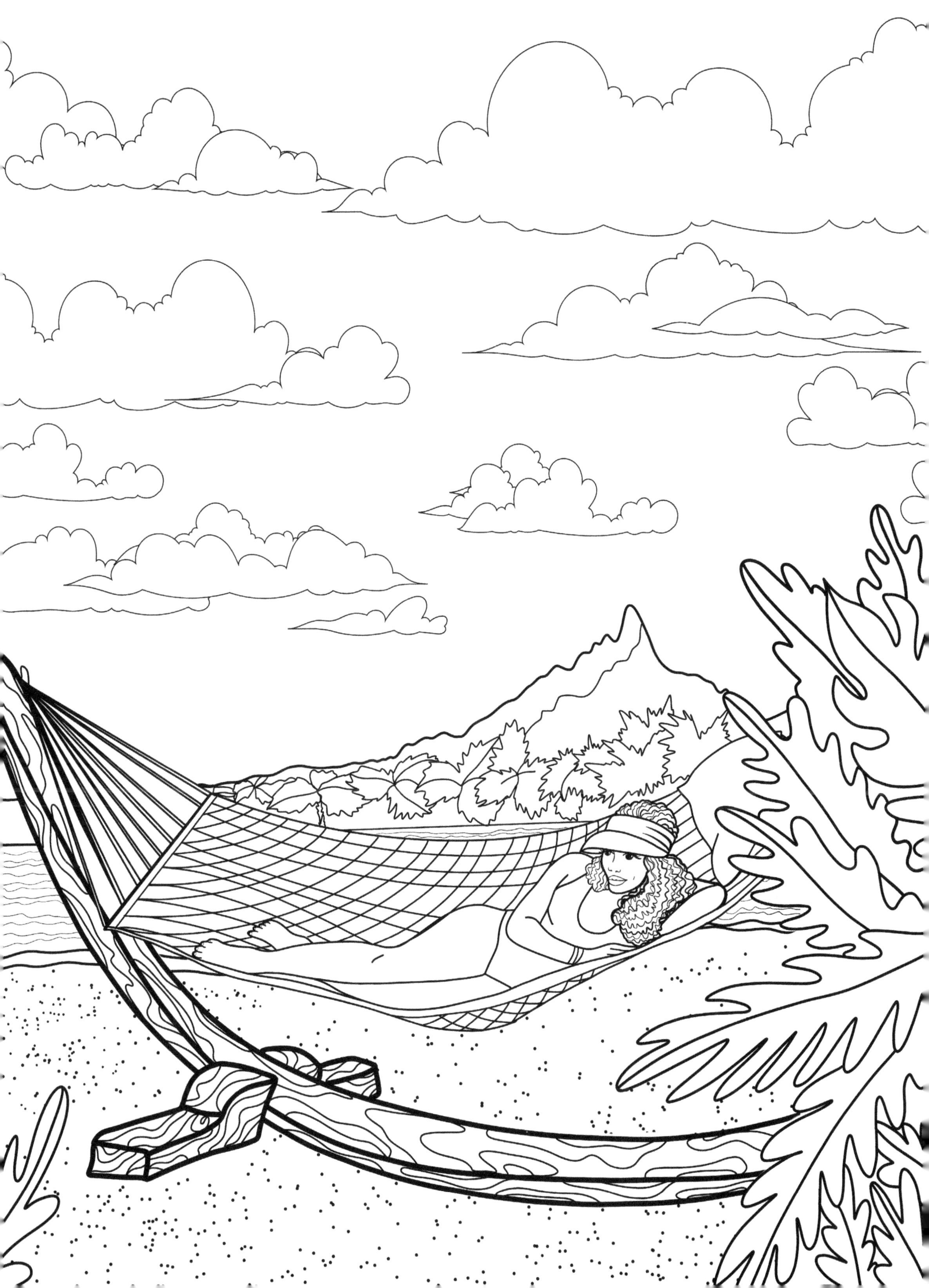

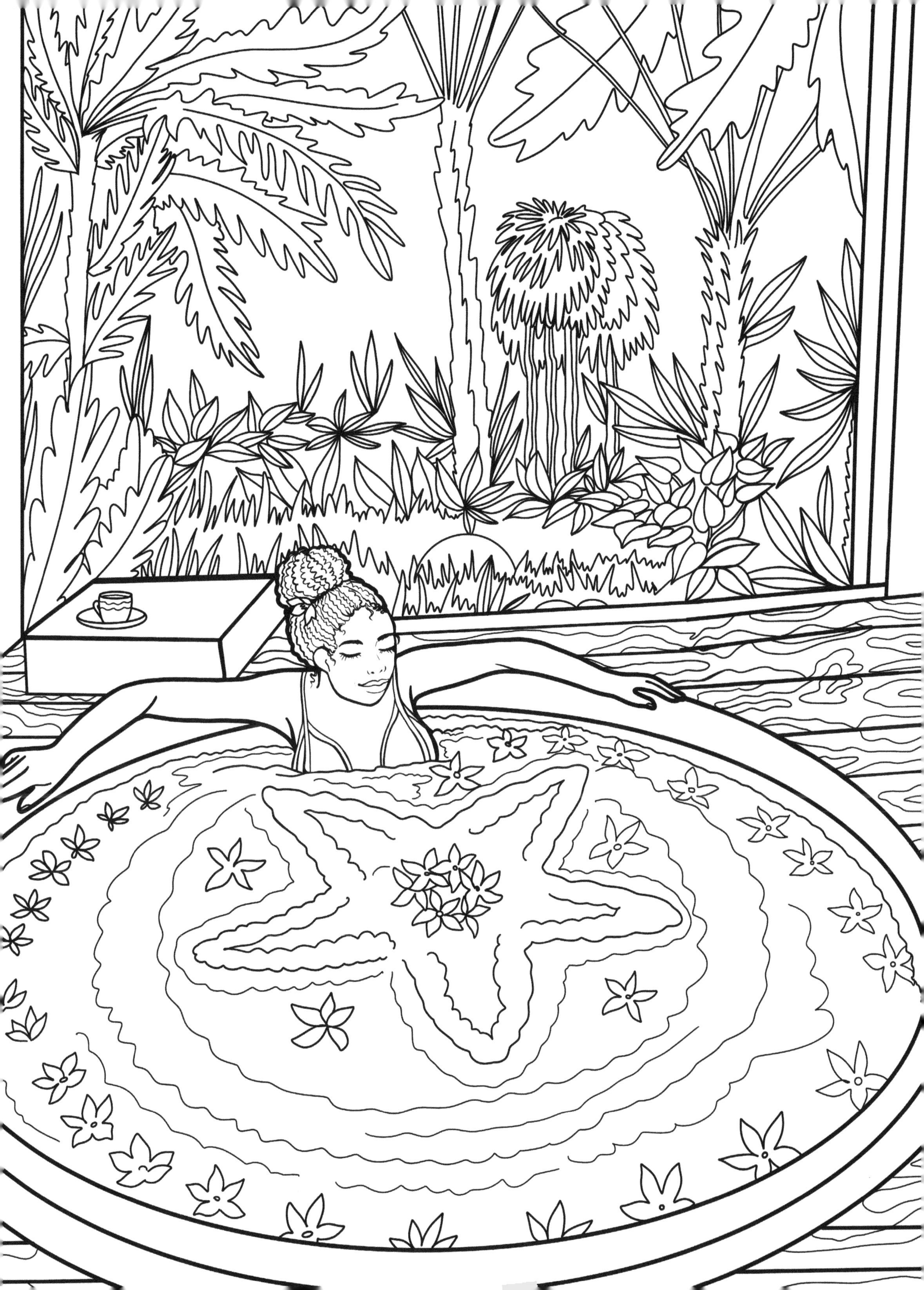

About the Author

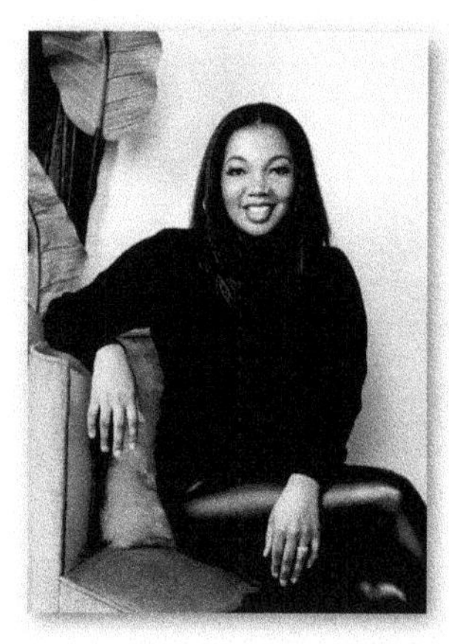

Shayla McGhee
Shayla McGhee resides in Atlanta, Georgia with her husband and three children. In her spare time, she enjoys writing, traveling, and spending time with her family and friends.

Find out more about Shayla's other works by following her on Instagram @shaylatmcghee or visiting sableinspiredbooks.com.

www.sableinspiredbooks.com **Facebook: @sableinspiredbooks** **Instagram: @sableinspiredbooks**

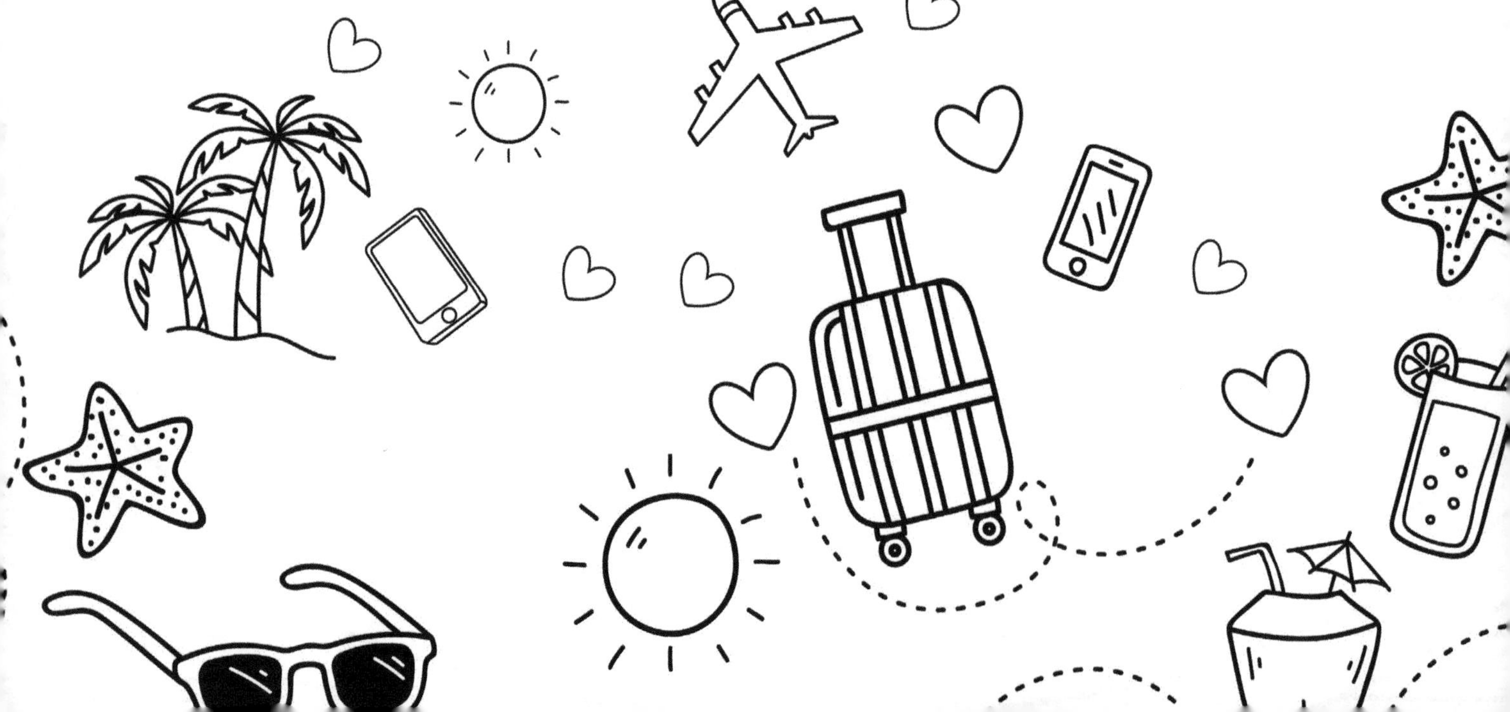

www.ingramcontent.com/pod-product-compliance
Ingram Content Group UK Ltd.
Pitfield, Milton Keynes, MK11 3LW, UK
UKHW051136260726
13967UKWH00010B/3082